8 ELEVEN-ARMED
LE SEA URC... 24
IBER 32 AUSTRA-
RAB 40 ELEPHANT
LIED SEAHORSE 56
NGED OCTOPUS 64
72 PORT JACKSON
IGUIN 88 WARATAH
ER-SPINED PORCU-
OUTHERN BISCUIT
Y SEADRAGON 120

CHRIS HUMFREY'S
INCREDIBLE COASTAL CRITTERS

To view the videos scan the QR codes with your phone or go to **newhollandpublishers.com/coastal** and enter the unique codes

CHRIS HUMFREY'S
INCREDIBLE COASTAL CRITTERS

The fascinating wildlife of Australia's seashores and rockpools, from sharks and penguins to porcupinefish and seadragons

PHOTOGRAPHS BY JAY TOWN

CONTENTS

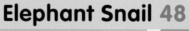

Introduction

Welcome into my fascinating world of Australian marine wildlife. Amazingly my earliest childhood memory was of seeing a seal swimming in the ocean at Phillip Island, Victoria. I have always marvelled at the extraordinary beauty of all creatures, and the brilliant jobs each species has in maintaining healthy ecosystems.

Luckily for me, I grew up with a very supportive mum and dad who helped nurture my wonderment for all things wild. When I was a kid, I had a veritable zoo in my very own backyard. My love and thirst for knowledge led me to study a Bachelor of Science at the University of Melbourne, majoring in Zoology and Botany. Today, I own and operate my very own private zoo, and I live with more than 2,000 animals, many of which are rare and endangered.

I have always been mesmerised and fascinated by the ocean. This foreign watery world is filled with many weird and wonderful inhabitants. Not only that, but our seas are essential to our very existence. For example, did you know that at least half the planet's oxygen which we breathe is derived from oceans? It makes me so sad that people treat the ocean just like one big toilet.

Join me in exploring the captivating underwater world of Australia's shorelines. Discover some remarkable creatures and learn about each animal's classification, adaptations, habitat, environment and ecological niche, plus loads of quirky fun facts. You'll be amazed to discover that some of these incredible ocean creatures live along the rocky shorelines of many of Australia's major cities.

Remember, education is the key to conservation. Let's all do something small in order to make a big positive impact on the natural world in which we live. If we study, learn and develop an understanding and empathy for all creatures, we are more likely to want to protect and conserve all species. I hope this book encourages you to get out and explore the natural world, to be safe and have fun! Are you ready to take a walk – or a dip – on the wild side?

Chris Humfrey,
Zoologist

Brown Sea Algae

Phaeophyta

'Certainly not a weed, this is an important plant-like species which we all need.'

Macro algae or 'seaweeds' belong to the kingdom Protista – they are plant-like aquatic **photosynthetic** organisms. Simply, that means they use sunlight to create nutrients from carbon dioxide and water, and oxygen is the by-product.

Superficially, they look like plants, however unlike higher plants they are not differentiated into roots, stems and leaves, and are without complex reproductive organs. These 'seaweeds' do not have flowers or pollen. Tiny algae and macro algae (seaweed) have nine times more biomass than plants on land and produce at least 50 per cent of the world's **oxygen**. Possibly the figure may be as high as 70 per cent.

Not only do macro algae provide shelter and refuge for many marine creatures to hide from predators and reproduce – they have such a vital job of removing carbon dioxide from the atmosphere and transforming it into life-supporting oxygen.

Some macro algae are the primary food source for animals at the bottom of the food chain, such as small shrimp-like creatures called **krill**, which are important food sources for larger marine animals including whales, penguins and other seabirds.

People rely on healthy sustainable populations of macro algae for food, pharmaceuticals and even sustainable clothing and footwear!

WOW, that's such a HUGE important job to do – they really are the trees of the oceans, acting as an important carbon sink and producing wonderful oxygen.

That's right, a biodegradable shoe has already been produced called the 'AlgiKicks'... and it's comprised of kelp.

Remember, it is vital to protect every species in an ecosystem, not just your favourites.

What's in a name?

Collectively, most people call brown macro algae 'seaweed'. However, they are not weeds at all. When we use the word 'weed' we are referring to an invasive pest which causes detrimental damage.

Sea algae release life-preserving oxygen into the ocean water via photosynthesis, helping to maintain biodiversity and protecting all marine life. Many sea algae are vital food sources for herbivorous marine animals such as molluscs, crustaceans, echinoderms and fish.

So, don't call them seaweeds – they are vital with very valuable jobs.

There are so many species which rely on sea algae as a food source, even people!

The various colours of macro algae are directly related to how sunlight changes as it passes through seawater. When it passes through water, light is split into a collection of rainbow colours: red, orange, yellow, green, blue, indigo and violet. Light at the red end of the spectrum does not penetrate below a 10-metre depth. Red and brown macro algae have developed red colour accessory pigments (rhodophycin) and brown (fucoxanthin) which hide the green of the chlorophyll and help assist with better photosynthesis at greater depths in the ocean.

Where are they found?

Brown sea algae are found along all Australian rocky shores and down to great depths in the ocean.

Why so many colours... green, red and brown?

Did you know that the study of algae is called PHYCOLOGY?

11

Amazing adaptations and morphology

There are three major types of macro marine algae: green, red and brown.

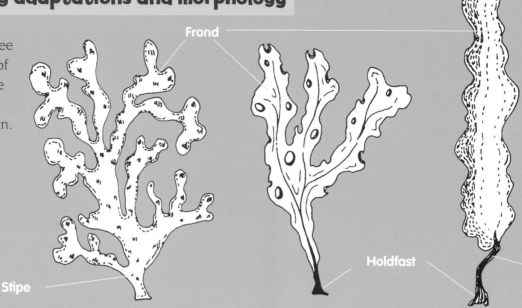

Frond

Stipe

Holdfast

Stipe

Green Algae

Brown Algae

Red Algae

Some brown algae species are farmed for enhancing flavours in European and Asian dishes, and they are also used as thickeners and emulsifiers. They are used in foods such as chewing gum, lollies and ice cream, and in toothpaste.

Sea algae is highly variable in colour, ranging from olive to yellow-brown to almost black.

> Who would have thought... you have more than likely eaten macro algae and you didn't even know it!

Brown macro algae species come in many different shapes and sizes. An abundant species often called 'Neptune's necklace', *Hormosira banksia* is a common sight adorning rocks at low tides along southern rocky shores; it is rich in iodine.

Some of the larger species of **kelp** can grow up to 30 metres and are often found washed up on sandy shores. Kelps are hardy, and are adapted for tough conditions; their thick waxy body is called the **thallus**. Each thallus is comprised of a **frond** and a **holdfast**. The holdfast superficially looks like tree roots and acts as an anchor to grip onto rocks to withstand being 'uprooted' by ferocious and wild seas. Unlike land plants, these holdfasts do not supply the plant with nutrients for growth.

The entire frond of the plant aids energy production for the process of photosynthesis.

Hey, they are like floaties in the baby pool!

The slimy feeling when touching some brown macro algae is a fabulous sensation – they feel like a slimy rubber gumboot.

Everyone is familiar with brown kelp washed up on the seashore. When it starts to decompose it sure can stink – YUK!

The frond of the kelp exudes a mucus which protects the algae from smashing against rocks in turbulent water. It also helps to protect the plant from the desiccating sun during low-tide exposure.

Some brown macro algae have gas-filled floating devices on the end of their fronds. These assist in maximising exposure to sunlight, which enhances photosynthesis.

Fronds of bull kelp are farmed on King Island in Bass Strait and used for the manufacture of **alginates**, which are very important in the pharmaceutical industry. They are used in a huge range of products, from make-up to dressings for wounds.

Did you know that alginates are used to coat fruit and vegetables as a barrier to bacteria?

Life cycle

There is so much that scientists have yet to learn about the life cycle of macro algae. We do know that macro algae reproduce more like ferns, which release spores or gametophytes. The spores can be either male or female, and they fuse with each other – this is known as gametogenesis. A sporophyte or young algae develops and grows into a mature macro algae. Some macro algae reproduce vegetatively, which means that they can clone themselves!

Check out the diagram: Brown macro algae really do have a fascinating reproductive life cycle – it's like something out of a sci-fi movie.

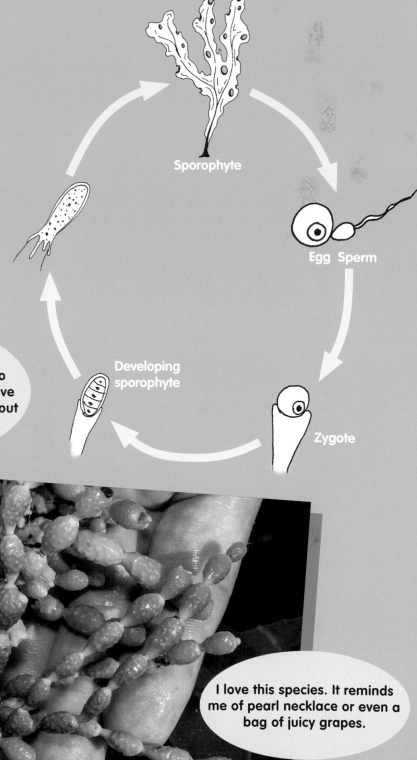

Sporophyte

Egg Sperm

Zygote

Developing sporophyte

I love this species. It reminds me of pearl necklace or even a bag of juicy grapes.

Predators and threats

Macro algae face many pressures. They are consumed by a myriad of herbivorous organisms in our oceans and face additional pressure from people-related factors such as habitat disturbance, farming for food, nutrient and sediment runoff, and climate change, as well as invasive species, all of which negatively impact on the abundance of healthy macro algae.

What can we do to help macro algae?

Ensure that we protect our wonderful oceans from human waste and pollution, which directly impacts on the health of macro algae.

Eleven-armed Seastar

Don't call them a starfish around me, that's almost like a swear word to a zoologist!

Coscinasterias muricata

'Don't call it a starfish – that's my wish.'

Although these creatures usually have 11 arms, the number of arms may vary from 7 to 14!

They would be awesome at playing table tennis.

Eleven-armed Seastars are predators. They are carnivorous and they love meat, consuming small crustaceans, molluscs and smaller seastars. They keep the balance in our amazing rockpool ecosystems.

They are like the 'Lion King' of our intertidal rocky shores.

Classification

KINGDOM:	Animalia
PHYLUM:	Echinodermata
CLASS:	Asteroidea
ORDER:	Forcipulatida
FAMILY:	Asteriidae
GENUS:	*Coscinasterias*
SPECIES:	*muricatus*

What's in a name?

Seastars are not fish at all and belong to the ancient phylum Echinodermata.

> That sounds like 'echidna', and they are certainly spiked like one too.

The meaning of echinoderm can be broken down into **echino** meaning 'spiky' in ancient Greek and **derm** meaning 'skin' in Latin.

> You certainly can't argue with that as they definitely have spiky skin.

Where is it found?

This amazing marine species is found along the coastline from Western Australia, through South Australia, Victoria, Tasmania and New South Wales, all the way to southern Queensland. It can be found as deep as 150 metres below the surface.

Amazing adaptations and morphology

Eleven-armed Seastars have exceptional camouflage. Each individual can be highly variable in colour, expertly blending in against a background of rocky crags or the sea floor.

Seastars have **radial symmetry**, which means that their arms are arranged evenly around a central disc – like the spokes on a BMX bike wheel!

Eleven-armed Seastars have very hard skin. For protection from hungry predators, they are covered in large spines surrounded by bony tubercles.

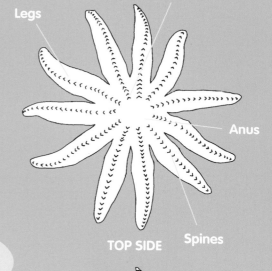

Central disc

Legs

Anus

Spines

TOP SIDE

> They really look like they are wearing army fatigues.

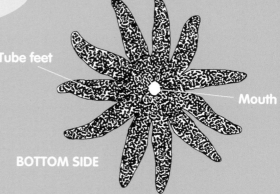

Tube feet

Mouth

BOTTOM SIDE

> You'd think twice about eating an Eleven-armed Seastar – you would get prickles in your mouth and need a throat lozenge.

The Eleven-armed seastar doesn't have any eyes, brain or central nervous system. However, it is equipped with sensory organs on the tip of each arm for sensing light and dark. These are called **eyespots**.

Seastars belong to the phylum Echinodermata. They don't have vertebrae; instead, their **endoskeleton** is made up of bony plates of calcium carbonate held together by strong flexible tissue in the epidermis (skin).

Light-sensitive Eleven-armed Seastars are mostly active at night. Species which are active at night are called **nocturnal**.

> Humans are diurnal – however mum and dad might beg to differ with you, watching Netflix on a Saturday night!

It has the amazing ability to grow new body parts. If an Eleven-armed Seastar loses its arm, it can grow another.

Boy oh boy, I wish we could do that!

Eleven-armed Seastars have **tube feet** inside their arms. Water is transported in and out of these tube feet like tiny jets to help with locomotion, and also to help the seastar to remain in one position if seas and currents are turbulent. Some seastar species have up to 15,000 tube feet!

Wow, imagine all of the socks you would have to wear – and pairing them back up again!

The tube feet are arranged in grooves along the arms; they operate under hydraulic pressure and are used to pass food through to the mouth, as well as to attach the seastar to solid surfaces, lever, grab, or propel it forward.

As an Eleven-armed Seastar's mouth is quite tiny, it can start digesting its food outside the body. To do this it spits its stomach out of its mouth to begin the digestion process – YUK!

Hey, that's disgusting table manners.

These seastars certainly do live in a 'topsy-turvy world' – their mouths are on their bottoms and the bottom is on the top!

An Eleven-armed Seastar's outer skin is covered in many tiny pincer-like snapping appendages called **pedicellaria**. These are used to repel small enemies and to collect food.

Amazingly, these seastars can **regrow a severed arm**! Often they are found with arms of differing lengths and sizes. The long arms are the older ones, whereas the shorter smaller emerging arms are the newer ones.

It's like something out of a Transformers movie.

Life cycle

Unbelievably, Eleven-armed Seastars can reproduce in two very different ways!

Male and female seastars can release their reproductive cells into the water, this is known as **spawning**. When the cells fuse together, seastar larvae can be produced!

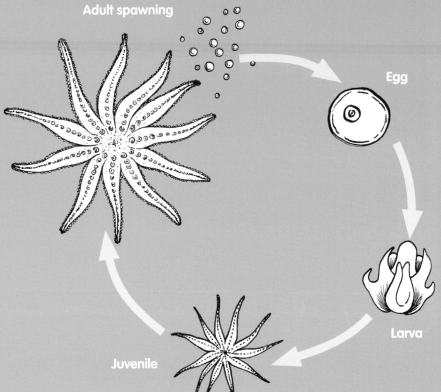

Adult spawning

Egg

Larva

Juvenile

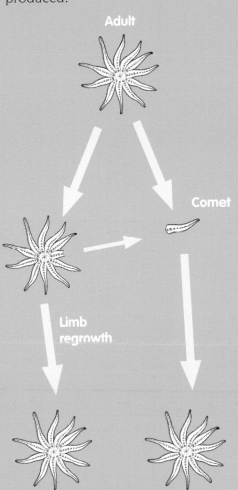

Adult

Comet

Limb regrowth

Clone adults

Seastars also have the ability reproduce without releasing their reproductive cells. A seastar can discard one of its many arms – this arm is called a **comet**. New legs start to grow from the newly formed central disc to make a new seastar. This seastar is a **clone** of the parent seastar, which will regrow the limb which it lost.

WOW, isn't that amazing?

Predators and threats

Eleven-armed Seastars do have some predators. Fish, rays, snails, crabs and even birds will eat them.

These seastars rely on clean seawater to survive. They live by incorporating seawater into their bodies in order to power their tube feet, support their body cavity, and provide circulation and a multitude of other basic bodily functions. If oceans and intertidal rocky shores are polluted with human waste and chemicals, this will adversely affect the seastars' health.

How can we help Eleven-armed Seastars?

I'm so glad that you asked!

Please ensure that you recycle all household litter and plastic waste, so it doesn't escape into storm water and out into our oceans.

Use biodegradable household products, which cause less harm to the environment.

When visiting the beach, always walk your dog on a lead, and if it decides to use the 'doggy-bathroom', pick up its poo, to ensure that we keep our beaches and intertidal rocky shores free from pollutants that detrimentally affect our amazing marine wildlife.

Look but don't touch! Enjoy rockpool rambling with family and friends together. However, always spare a thought for our rockpool denizens. Please don't stress them out. Admire them from afar – and marvel at their truly fascinating lives.

SCAN HERE
to watch a WILD clip

hjersm

23

Purple Sea Urchin

Heliocidaris erythrogramma

'Spiky and grand, it looks like a hairdo from an eighties rock band!'

Remarkably adaptive, this sea urchin species lives at every depth and in a wide variety of habitats and temperatures. Their body looks like a pincushion with moveable spines, and they are covered with a five-plated shell covered with a thin skin.

Sea urchins do a wonderful job by keeping our coastlines clean from algae build-up. They are also a very important part of the food chain.

Classification

KINGDOM:	Animalia
PHYLUM:	Echinodermata
CLASS:	Echinoidea
ORDER:	Echinoida
FAMILY:	Echinomeridae
GENUS:	*Heliocidaris*
SPECIES:	*erythrogramma*

What's in a name?

We already know that **echinoderm** means 'spiky skin'. For the genus names *helio* translates as 'sun' and *cidaris* means 'tiara' or 'crown', while for the species name *erythros* means 'reddish colour'.

Purple Sea Urchins are **echinoderms** (sounds like 'eee-k-eye-no-derms'), so they have lots of spikes all over their **exoskeletons** and thousands of **tube feet** under their bodies.

Their bodies are dome shaped and can be a few different colours, including dark green and pink. The Purple Sea Urchin is mostly reddish-purple in colour.

Where is it found?

Purple Sea Urchins live on the **rocky coastlines** of southern Queensland, New South Wales, Victoria, Tasmania, South Australia and Western Australia. This is the most common sea urchin species in southern Australia.

Purple Sea Urchins live in **rockpools** or rocky shores on the coast. Rocks and rockpools help to keep them safe, by providing them with food and something to hold onto.

They can live as deep as 35 metres under the surface! They tend to prefer rocky areas with an abundance of macro algae, where they can seek shelter from turbulent conditions and predators.

Amazing adaptations and morphology

When sea urchins feel threatened, they bunch up together to look like one huge sea urchin that's too big to eat!

A sea urchin's anus is located on the top part if its body, and just like its cousin the seastar its mouth is located underneath.

Purple Sea Urchins have a sieve plate near the anus on the top part of the body. This porous area is very important as it transports water through the urchin vascular system. Everything the sea urchin does is controlled by this water vascular system, including moving its hydraulic-tube feet, eating, breathing and even excreting.

Sea urchins use their spines like 'chopsticks' to manipulate food down to the base of the mouth.

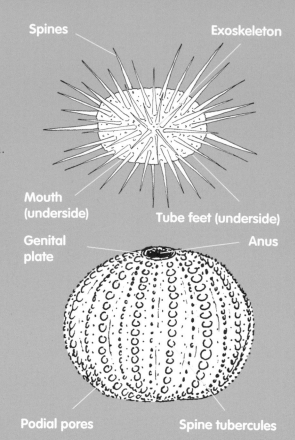

Spines

Exoskeleton

Mouth (underside)

Tube feet (underside)

Genital plate

Anus

Podial pores

Spine tubercules

It can maintain a constant water current throughout its body. WOW, that's clever for an animal with no brain.

Ha! Fancy having your mouth on your bottom, and your bottom on your head. Very funny.

I've even noticed that a sea urchin can cover itself in macro algae as camouflage – very clever.

Purple Sea Urchins can also use their spines to burrow into small spaces on rocks or into the sand to stay safe.

Some sea urchin species have venomous spines, but not the Purple Sea Urchin! Amazingly, each spine is attached to a ball joint known as a **tubercle**, which enables the sea urchin to independently move them and point them at a source of danger.

Sea urchins don't have eyes – instead they use their spines to help them to navigate and feel.

The sea urchin has a five-plated shell called a **test**. This hard-armoured plating protects the urchin. Long tube feet protrude through the channels of these plates. When sea urchins die their test is often washed up on shores.

Purple Sea Urchin tube feet are also handy multi-use tools. They use them to absorb oxygen, to eat, for touching, locomotion and expelling body waste. The suction cups at the end of the tube feet are called **podia** and they manipulate these to sense for chemicals in their environment.

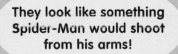

They look like something Spider-Man would shoot from his arms!

Protected among their moveable spines are small **pedicellariae**. These are used for grabbing food also for deterring parasites and pests that may wish to hitch a ride on the sea urchin.

Under a magnifying glass, these grabbing appendages look ferocious and nasty.

The mouth of a sea urchin is set in the middle of the underside of the body. It is equipped with a set of jaws and horny 'rasping' teeth. The five strong teeth are also called **pyramids** because of their shape. Although scary looking up-close, these teeth are primarily used for chewing and grinding away on algae.

The entire mouth area of the sea urchin is called **Aristotle's Lantern,** named after the famous philosopher who first studied this creature more than 2,000 years ago! Aristotle noted that a cross-section of a sea urchin's mouth region resembled a 'horn lantern' – a very popular light source during that period.

WOW, that really is a fascinating historical fact.

Sea urchins' favourite food is algae, but they also eat mussels, snails and worms. Eating both plants and animals means that they are **omnivorous**. They consume food just like seastars – by vomiting their stomachs out of their mouths!

Gross – that is disgusting table manners.

Sea urchins then secrete a digestive enzyme that turns their lunch into the equivalent of a smoothie. Finally, they suck their stomach and their liquid lunch back into their mouths!

Life cycle

Sea urchins are **oviparous** (sounds like 'oh-vip-ah-ros'), which means that they lay eggs. Sea urchins are broadcast spawners, where both the male and female sea urchin release reproductive cells in large clouds into the water en masse. Some female sea urchins can release several million eggs. Once the eggs are fertilised, they begin to grow and develop.

When the eggs hatch the babies are called **embryos.** These embryos keep growing into **larvae** with four arms, so we call them four-arm larvae!

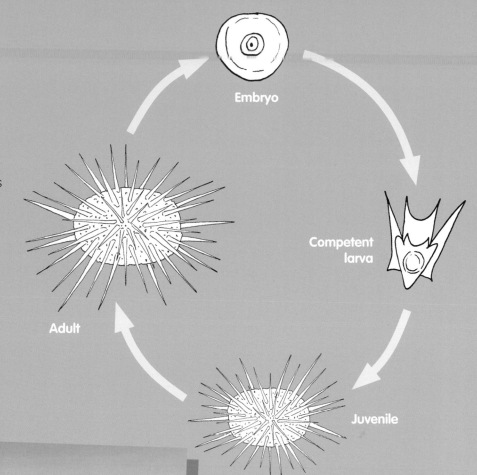

Embryo

Competent larva

Adult

Juvenile

These larvae keep growing into six-arm larvae, but six still isn't enough arms to be an urchin ... yet. They keep growing until they start to make an **exoskeleton** that supports more spines, then they become **juveniles**.

Purple Sea Urchins can live up to 20 years of age!

Predators and threats

Not many creatures would be brave enough to eat an urchin, but some that do include lobsters, crabs, large fish and seals.

People from many cultures worldwide relish eating sea urchins. However, the only edible parts of a sea urchin are the reproductive organs, the gonads.

I have eaten them myself, however I think that they must be an acquired taste!

Because urchins are so highly prized as a delicacy they sadly are 'overfished' in many locations. On the southern coastlines of Australia, it is illegal to collect sea urchins from certain areas. Heavy penalties apply if these laws are not observed.

How can we help sea urchins?

If you are exploring rockpools and intertidal regions, be careful to 'tread lightly'. It's always best to look but not touch.

Report to the authorities any unscrupulous over collecting of this amazing echinoderm.

Human waste, run off and petrochemicals all harm Purple Sea Urchin populations.

Remember, if you are at the beach with your pet dog, please pick up its poo!

SCAN HERE
to watch a WILD clip

vimitu

Brown Sea Cucumber

Australostichopus mollis

'A very peculiar-looking creature indeed.'

It looks like something you would find left behind by a pooch on a nature strip.

KINGDOM:	Animalia
PHYLUM:	Echinodermata
CLASS:	Holothuroidea
ORDER:	Synallactida
FAMILY:	Stichopodidae
GENUS:	*Australostichopus*
SPECIES:	*mollis*

What's in a name?

The Brown Sea Cucumber is also known as the Soft Sea Cucumber. There are more than 1,700 described species of sea cucumbers worldwide, many of them quite colourful and beautiful. However, the Brown Sea Cucumber is a rather 'unflattering' mission-brown colour, possibly to help camouflage it against the silty ocean floor where it lives.

The Brown Sea Cucumber is the only species in the genus *Australostichopus* and it could possibly become an important species for the fisheries industry in years to come.

The ancient Greek philosopher Aristotle was the first person to the use the word **Holothuroidea** to name the class to which sea cucumbers belong. **Holos** means 'whole' and *thurious* means 'rushing'.

The species name *mollis* means 'soft' in ancient Greek.

It's not a vegetable that you can buy from the greengrocers, it's an animal – and a very peculiar creature indeed.

That's a little odd, I wouldn't say that they were the fastest creature in the sea.

That makes a lot of sense. They feel like a gherkin in a pickle jar.

Where is it found?

These sea cucumbers live in depths ranging from 20 metres to 200 metres along the coasts of the southern half of Australia. They are also found along the coasts of New Zealand's North and South Islands.

Brown Sea Cucumbers can be found under rocks and in sandy areas. Unlike other sea cucumber species, they live on hard surfaces and are less inclined to burrow. Sea cucumbers are generally **nocturnal**.

What a weird looking animal!

Amazing adaptations and morphology

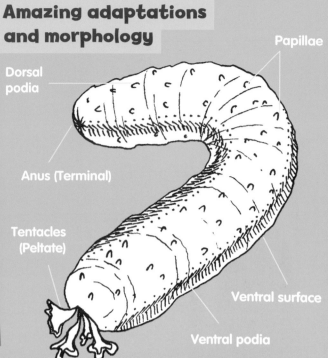

Dorsal podia

Papillae

Anus (Terminal)

Tentacles (Peltate)

Ventral surface

Ventral podia

Members of this sea cucumber species have two gonads (reproductive organs) present internally – one on each side of the cylindrical body.

The Brown Sea Cucumber is one of the largest species in the Holothuroid family found in Victoria, growing up to 20 centimetres in length and covered in conical papillae with tube feet along their undersides. The tentacles grow from around the mouth and have disc-shaped, 'leaf-like' tips. Their colour varies from pale brown to mottled greys and black. The juveniles are often white, which originally led to scientists mistakenly classifying them as a different species!

Sea cucumbers move around by using the tube feet on their undersides. The tube feet are called **podia** and are connected to the **water vascular system**, which works like a skeleton by keeping fluid pressure throughout the body and helping the animal maintain its shape. Sea cucumbers also have thick sheets of body-wall muscles that help support the body structure.

Sea cucumbers use their tentacles to catch their prey in a method called **suspension feeding**. They hold up the tentacle located around their mouth and secrete a mucus from the papillae to catch floating organic particles and plankton.

The Brown Sea Cucumber is a **detritivore**, devouring literally any organic matter.

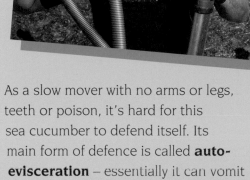

> It's like a vacuum cleaner, consuming all the organic waste.

As a slow mover with no arms or legs, teeth or poison, it's hard for this sea cucumber to defend itself. Its main form of defence is called **auto-evisceration** – essentially it can vomit up its intestines in an attempt to deter potential predators from eating it!

> That is so disgusting! Don't worry, they can grow back the intestines again.

Unlike their cousins the seastars, sea cucumbers lack radial symmetry – instead they retain the **bilateral symmetry** of their larval stage. The Brown Sea Cucumber has a definite front end and back end, compared to a seastar with a top and bottom.

The Brown Sea Cucumber absorbs oxygen with its highly vascularised anus.

> That is so unique and amazing – a bottom-breathing sea cucumber.

> Hey! A bum-breathing animal. Ha ha!

Life cycle

Sea cucumbers are not hermaphrodites – that means there are two distinct genders, male and female.

Eggs spawning

Adult

Juvenile

Reproduction events are timed by the lunar cycle and often happen after a full moon. The males and females release their reproductive cells into the ocean in a **spawning** event. The eggs that are fertilised do not grow immediately into a sea cucumber, but rather go through several larval life stages.

The larval life stages are **planktonic** and free floating in the ocean. The first stage is called an **auricularia**, the second stage a **doliolaria**, and the final stage a **pentactula**. After the pentactula stage the larva drops down to the ocean floor to continue developing.

Brown Sea Cucumbers are **detritivores**. That means they eat the remnants of everyone else's meals! From floating organisms to organic matter on the ocean floor, these sea cucumbers are not fussy.

Predators and threats

Sea cucumbers are sometimes eaten by seastars and large predatory molluscs. Apart from that, they have no known predators.

Brown Sea Cucumbers are very common in Australia and New Zealand with stable populations. However, in other areas of the world, including much of Asia and the South Pacific, they are considered a food item for humans and are at risk from overfishing.

Sea cucumbers are considered a delicacy in many countries, especially in Asia. A kilogram of sea cucumber can fetch an exorbitant price of $3,000.

Pharmaceutical companies are investigating the Chinese medicinal benefits of sea cucumbers.

SCAN HERE
to watch a WILD clip

lrjlzx

Australian Land Hermit Crab

Coenobita variabilis

This hermit crab plays a vital role in cleaning up intertidal ecosystems.

'A plucky crab that likes to grab.'

The Australian Land Hermit Crab is omnivorous and lives on a diet of meat, fruit and vegetable matter!

Hermit crabs are vital scavengers for our oceans worldwide. They help clean up the mess by consuming decaying organic waste. They are also a vital food source for many other species, making them an integral part of food webs.

41

Classification

KINGDOM:	Animalia
PHYLUM:	Arthropoda
CLASS:	Malacostraca
ORDER:	Decapoda
FAMILY:	Coenobitidae
GENUS:	*Coenobita*
SPECIES:	*variabilis*

What's in a name?

The Australian Land Hermit Crab belongs to the Class Malacostraca. In Ancient Greek, **malakos** means 'soft' and **ostracon** means 'shell'. This may sound a little confusing, as these crabs only have soft shells after they have moulted their skin.

The order Decapoda refers to the hermit crab's ten legs (five pairs). **Deca** means 'ten' and **poda** means 'foot'.

The Australian Land Hermit Crab belongs to the family of crabs called Coenobitidae. In Ancient Greek **coeno** means 'together' or 'commune', and this certainly reflects this species' habit of being found together in large communities.

> What a great idea – safety in numbers – you have less chance of being picked off by a predator.

The name 'hermit' crab is really a misnomer. Although this little crustacean lives alone in a shell, they are often very social and congregate with others.

Where is it found?

There are thought to be more than 800 different species of hermit crabs worldwide; some live on land, while others have an aquatic lifestyle. The Australian Land Hermit Crab favours warm tropical shores of Northern Territory, Queensland and the northern coasts of New South Wales and Western Australia.

Amazing adaptations and morphology

Hermit crabs belong to the phylum Arthropoda, which means that they have an exoskeleton, a segmented body and jointed limbs.

As hermit crabs grow bigger, they moult or shed their skin. This is known as **ecdysis**.

Hermit crabs have the amazing ability to live on land. To do this they carry a supply of water inside their shell, which allows them to breathe and also helps them to keep cool and hydrated.

Hermit crabs have two pairs of **antennae**, which they use to navigate and to sense for food and danger.

They don't have to go to the shops to buy clothes – that's way cheaper than buying new threads.

The antennae remind of the old-fashioned TV aerial for picking up a signal.

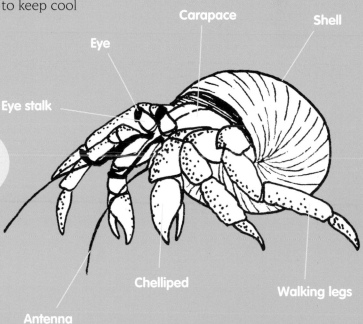

Eye

Carapace

Shell

Eye stalk

Chelliped

Antenna

Walking legs

Interestingly, there is a rather sinister side to the cute and humble-looking hermit crab. It does not form or create its shell. Instead, it steals it from a mollusc (after eating it) or fortuitously discovers an empty shell and moves in. Spare shells are hot property for hermit crabs, and many a rumble and squabble can arise from crabs competing for the same shell. Hermit crabs have even been known to fight to the death for hotly contested real estate.

That's tough. Haven't they heard of an auction?

No bills, no rent – WOW, they are always on holidays. I want to be a hermit crab!

Without the fortified protection of a mollusc's vacated shell, the Australian Land Hermit Crab would be defenceless against predators.

The hermit crab has periscopic eyestalks, enabling it to survey its immediate environment from the safety of its hard fortified home. This adaptation is extremely useful for watching out for danger.

That's like a periscope on a submarine – so cool!

Hermit crabs possess eyes which can see both ultraviolet and visible light, allowing them to see equally well both by day and night. They tend to be more active at night, away from the eyes of hungry predators.

In addition to the hard outer shell, the crab's claws offer protection against predators, while they also use them to hunt prey.

The abdomen of the hermit crab is soft and lacks the hard exoskeleton of the cephalothorax. The asymmetric abdomen has a basal hook on the end so that the crab can squeeze into and grip the grooves of the shell using its abdominal muscles. As the hermit grows bigger, they outgrow their 'digs' and are forced to move out to find a larger living space.

Some hermit crab species can remodel and groove out the inside of the vacated mollusc shell, making it larger.

Did you know that an animal which is active during both daytime and at night is called CATHEMERAL?

That's like doing a house renovation so that you don't have to look for a new place – very clever!

The Australian Land Hermit Crab has a segmented body and ten jointed legs. The front legs are modified into claws known as chelae. The larger left claw is used for defence and warding off danger, while the smaller right claw is generally purposed for scooping water and food.

The second and third pairs of legs are used for walking, while hermit crabs are surprisingly great climbers! The fourth and fifth pairs of legs are used to grip onto the column of the shell which they live in, protecting the vulnerable soft abdomen.

These little crabs mean business and will give you a nasty pinch if you mess around with them.

That's kind of like grappling hooks, or an anchor on a ship.

Life cycle

The life cycle of these hermit crabs is quite complex and fascinating. A male and female will meet and face the openings of each other's shells. Both will partially remove themselves from the safe confines of their shells, so that the male can pass on reproductive cells to the female.

This romantic encounter can make them susceptible to attack from a hungry predator.

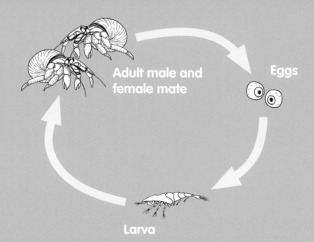

Adult male and female mate

Eggs

Larva

Fertilised eggs develop into tiny, free-swimming larvae called **zoea**. Zoea grow and moult several times before becoming symmetrical **megalops**, which are still miniature but have developed into a crustacean-like form. Megalops moult and grow into juvenile hermit crabs.

The size of the female hermit crab will directly affect how many eggs she will lay. Larger females lay more eggs than smaller ones, and the exact figure can be anywhere between 800 and 50,000 eggs in one event.

Woah, that's a lot of brothers and sisters to fight over the remote control with!

I love the word megalops, it means 'large eyes' in ancient Greek.

Only a tiny percentage of the thousands of eggs will develop into adulthood. Just like many ocean inhabitants, the reproductive strategy of producing multitudes of young, and only a few surviving, contributes to the richness of pelagic plankton consisting of larval organisms which larger animals depend on for nutrients and survival.

Plankton really is a nutrient-rich soup for so many animals to eat. It shows how every species is interconnected. Without the smaller, less obvious creatures, the larger more charismatic filter-feeding animals such as whales wouldn't be able to survive.

Predators and threats

Hermit crabs face many perils in Australia's rocky shores. Gulls, terns and shorebirds such as oystercatchers view them as a tasty snack. Multitudes of fish species, larger echinoderms and octopus would gorge themselves on hermit crabs.

Hermit crabs always need to be on the lookout for danger.

How can we help hermit crabs?

Hermit crab species are commonly seen in rockpools and intertidal zones throughout Australia.

Please don't be tempted to pick one up and take it home as a pet – it will most likely perish.

If you are wanting to keep a land hermit crab as a pet, please do your homework, and be a diligent hermit-crab carer.

Like most marine species, human litter, waste and pollution negatively affect intertidal ecosystems.

Next time you are visiting the beach, tread lightly, take home your rubbish, wear environmentally friendly sunscreen, and pick up your dog's poo!

Australian children often keep Australian Land Hermit Crabs as pets. Sadly, these crabs are sourced from the wild and are not bred in captivity. The collection of these animals for the pet trade is simply unsustainable. Hermit crabs can be very difficult to keep alive in captivity if best-practice husbandry for this animal is not applied. Although hermit crabs can live up to 20 years in captivity, most pet hermit crabs brought home as pets only live for a month of two. They are sadly known as 'throw-away' pets.

SCAN HERE
to watch a WILD clip

nfucfn

Elephant Snail

Scutus antipodes

'Now you see me, now you don't.'

This midnight-black cryptic sea snail spends its life beneath the sea grazing on marine algae like an underwater cow!

It has super-long antennae which remind me of an ever-exploring elephant's trunk.

Classification

KINGDOM:	Animalia
PHYLUM:	Mollusca
CLASS:	Gastropoda
ORDER:	Archaeogastropoda
FAMILY:	Fissurellidae
GENUS:	*Scutus*
SPECIES:	*antipodes*

What's in a name?

Just like the common Garden Snail found in backyards, the Elephant Snail belongs to the phylum Mollusca. Molluscs are a well-known invertebrate group of animals which include octopus, squid, snails, clams, tusk shells and chitons.

The skin feels like freshly chewed bubble gum.

Class **Gastropoda** refers to this animal's obvious morphological characteristics, with **gastro** meaning 'stomach' and **poda** meaning 'foot'.

The family name **Fissurellidae** refers to the slit-like fissure near the head which is the opening for respiration.

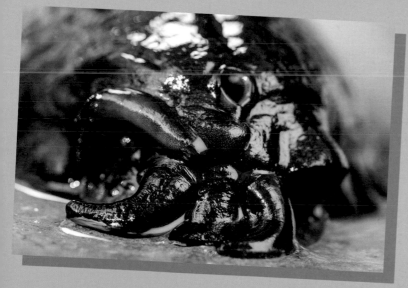

The genus name **Scutus** refers to the large, long white shell, which looks like a Roman shield and is used for protection. Elephant Snails belong to a group of snails also known as 'shield snails'.

The species name ***antipodes*** refers to the fact that this snail is found only on the 'other side of the world', meaning Australia to the European scientists who named it.

49

Where is it found?

The Elephant Snail can be commonly found in **intertidal zones** along the coasts of Queensland, New South Wales, Victoria, Tasmania and Western Australia.

It is commonly seen at low tide, seeking refuge in **rockpools** and inside rocky ledges and crevices up to 20 metres deep, staying safe from the prying eyes of hungry gulls.

Amazing adaptations and morphology

The Elephant Snail is often referred to as the **Elephant Slug** because of its unique stocky appearance. The jet-black muscular foot of the snail encompasses the white shell, giving the snail a slug-like appearance.

Next time you are at the beach, get down low and peer into some of the exposed rockpool caves – you'll be certain to see an Elephant Snail.

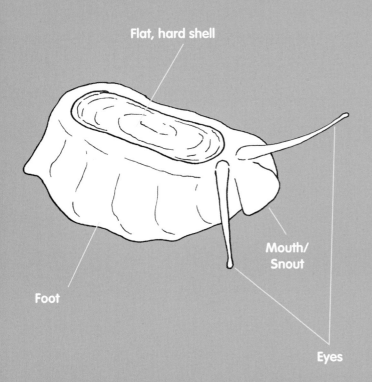

Flat, hard shell

Foot

Mouth/ Snout

Eyes

The strong muscular foot is a superb adaptation to help this snail survive the intertidal zone by anchoring itself firmly to rocks so that it doesn't dry out at low tide or become damaged in rough ocean conditions.

People have two feet, whereas the Elephant Snail only has one, so GASTROPOD makes sense – one stomach, one foot!

Its foot is like a giant suction cup holding on to the rocky substrate.

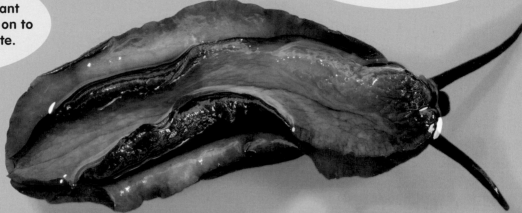

It is a member of the keyhole limpet family and is the largest of the Australian false limpits. It can grow up to a whopping **16 centimetres**, although snails just over half this length are more commonly observed.

The snail also has two mantle flaps that can extend over the top of the shell, almost or completely hiding the shell. This is a perfect adaptation for hiding on the dark rocky recesses on the intertidal zone.

That's like Harry Potter's cloak of invisibility.

The Elephant Snail has a protruding snout when viewed from underneath, and two long tentacles on the head. The tentacles are **chemosensory**, which enables the snail to differentiate between chemical signals in the water, helping them to find food and a mate, and assisting in avoiding predators.

When viewed from underneath the Elephant Snail has a very pronounced **snout**, almost like an elephant's trunk!

Inside the snout is a retractable **radula**, which is a bit like a tongue covered in small tooth-like structures. It is used for rasping away at algae and turning it into smaller particles for ingestion.

The Elephant Snail has a small opening around the head that is used for respiration. Water is drawn in and passes over the gills and then leaves via the same opening, collecting waste particles on the way out.

To move around the snail secretes a mucus that allows it to glide on its large muscular foot across various substrates.

It's one way in, and one way out!

That's like a self-made slippery dip.

The Elephant Snail's shell isn't like the shell of a familiar Garden Snail. Instead it is **shallow and broad** – an adaptation that reduces the resistance of the water flow while the snail is attached to rocky substrates in the often-turbulent waters of its intertidal habitat.

The **nocturnal** Elephant Snail is slow moving, preferring the cover of night to avoid predators while it searches for food.

Elephant Snails are **herbivorous** grazers, consuming many algae and soft coral. The snail's chemosensory antennae and radula help them to find and feast on algal growth on coral reefs and rocky outcrops.

Life cycle

Elephant Snails are **oviparous**, meaning that they produce eggs, and in this case, they are coated in jelly.

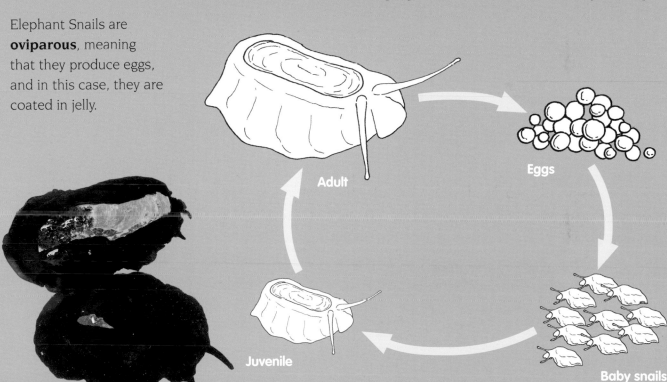

Adult

Eggs

Baby snails

Juvenile

Predators and threats

Elephant Snails can be eaten by a variety of marine predators including large fish and marine mammals. Historically, indigenous people relished eating this species, removing the soft black outer flesh and eating the muscular foot of the snail.

These snails are mostly common throughout their range and at present are not considered to be under threat. More research is needed to study how their status may alter due to climate change, ocean warming, acidification and pollution.

Elephant Snails play a vital role in intertidal ecosystems. Not only are they key herbivores maintaining macro-algal abundance, but at the same time they also assist in ecosystem stability.

This enigmatic mollusc is also an important **bio-indicator**. It requires undisturbed pollution-free intertidal zones in order to survive.

> Who would have thought that a small sea snail has such a HUGE important job to undertake?

> WOW, their presence tells us that the ocean is healthy and clean.

How can we help Elephant Snails?

Citizen science is a fabulous way to help monitor the health of our environment. Why not gather a group of family and friends together and safely go and explore your local intertidal zone. Record your observations and share this information with your local authorities and conservation groups.

SCAN HERE
to watch a WILD clip

wqhqfk

Pot-bellied Seahorse

Hippocampus abdominalis

'They don't eat hay, and you sure can't ride them at the Melbourne Cup'

There are more than 100 different species of seahorses worldwide. One of the largest, the Pot-bellied Seahorse, is found here in Australia.

This is certainly one of the most magical creatures living in the ocean.

Throughout history seahorses have captivated the imagination of people. They have been worn as talismans, used to ward off sickness, and to bring the wearer good fortune and health.

Did you know that sadly in some cultures the ashes from dead seahorses are sold as a remedy to cure baldness. Others believe that if eaten it can ward off rabies.

Every animal has a job to do, and seahorses are no exception. They are important predators of small crustaceans and form part of the food web for larger predators.

Also, they are super-cute!

Classification

KINGDOM:	Animalia
PHYLUM:	Chordata
CLASS:	Actinopterygii
ORDER:	Syngnathiformes
FAMILY:	Syngnathidae
GENUS:	*Hippocampus*
SPECIES:	*abdominalis*

What's in a name?

Superficially resembling a horse, this aquatic marvel of disguise is a fish and belongs to the class Actinopterygii. In ancient Greek *actino* means 'having rays' and *pterux* means 'wings' or 'fins' – simply translated this is the 'ray-finned fish'.

Seahorses, along with their cousins the seadragons and pipefish, belong to the family Syngnathidae. In ancient Greek, *syn* means 'together' and *gnathos* is a 'jaw', referring to this family of fishes' inability to open their jaws.

The genus name *Hippocampus* literally translates to *Hippo*, meaning 'horse', and *campos*, meaning monster. So seahorses are the '**horse-like sea monsters**'.

Don't you think it's weird that a part of the human brain is called the hippocampus. It must have taken one crazy brain-dissecting scientist to call it that!

Where is it found?

Pot-bellied Seahorses are found along the south-eastern coastlines of Australia, including around Tasmania, in waters up to 100 metres deep. This curious fish can also be found across the Tasman Sea in New Zealand. They live in algae or seagrass forests, along coral reefs or rocky outcrops, and attach to sponges or even jetties or ramps.

Amazing morphology and adaptations

A Pot-bellied Seahorse is not renowned for its swimming prowess; however, it does have some marvellous adaptations for survival.

This seahorse is adorned with a 'crown' called a **coronet** on the top of its head. The coronet is a unique identifier, being different on each individual seahorse.

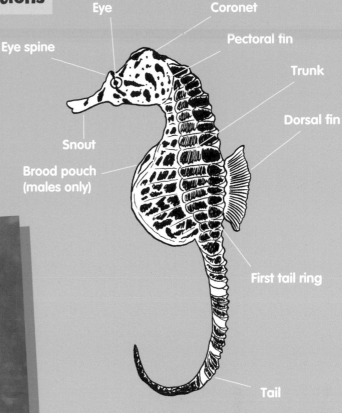

Eye
Coronet
Eye spine
Pectoral fin
Trunk
Dorsal fin
Snout
Brood pouch
(males only)
First tail ring
Tail

That's just like fingerprints with people.

The body is made up of interlocking bony, scaly **plates** that afford protection against predators.

WOW, they really do look like they are wearing a knight's armour – they would make a very crunchy meal for a predator.

59

The Pot-bellied Seahorse has pectoral fins directly behind its gills, with a large but weak dorsal fin on the back. It synchronises the oscillation rates of the dorsal and pectoral fins, enabling it to hover and manoeuvre expertly with fine precision.

WOW, the seahorse can oscillate its fins up to an amazing 35 times per second. They remind me of a hovering gyrocopter.

Seahorses are relatively weak swimmers. They rely on a long **prehensile** tail to anchor them to a structure in their chosen habitat; they then catch their prey as it floats past.

That's like a monkey using its tail to hang on to a branch.

Adult males are endowed with the big 'pot belly', while the females have a smaller ridged belly. The male's pot belly acts as a brood pouch for holding the incubating eggs and safeguarding tiny young.

Dad has a pouch, just like a female kangaroo does!

Inside the pouch the young are afforded fantastic protection from environmental change and predation.

A seahorse's snout is long, fused and has no teeth. It works like a vacuum sucking up prey.

This is a creature that certainly puts all of its eggs into one basket.

Having no teeth might sound like a tough gig, but these curious fish instead have a long snout that works just like a vacuum cleaner 'sssssssslurping' up their favourite food meal of small shrimps.

Their eyes are small, but seahorses have excellent vision, even being able to move their eyes independently of each other. That means they can keep one eye on their prey while the other one looks out for predators.

Pot-bellied Seahorses are **gender dimorphic**, so the males and females look a little different. Males tend to have more spikes and ornamentations on their heads.

It looks like they have used gel to make a mohawk hairdo.

A Pot-bellied Seahorse evades predators by hiding in among sea algae to camouflage itself.

They truly are masters of disguise.

Life cycle

Amazingly, parental roles are reversed. Seahorses and their close relatives are the only species where the **male will give birth** instead of the female.

Pot-bellied Seahorses can breed year-round, but their busiest season is usually spring and summer when the water temperature becomes warmer. Males perform a courtship dance aimed at attracting a female's attention. Sometimes multiple males will compete for one female's attention!

> The biggest, best dressed, jazziest dancer gets more attention from a would-be suitor.

Eggs grow and develop in the brood pouch of the male

Adult female transfers eggs to adult male

Male gives birth to somewhere between 12–1000 baby seahorses

Babies grow into adults

When the female has chosen her partner, she deposits more than 300 eggs into his brood pouch, where the male fertilises them and protects them until they hatch.

> The male then gives birth to the live young – we call this ovoviviparity.

The eggs take approximately four weeks to incubate. During this period a male will aerate water in the pouch, providing fresh water and nutrients for the embryos to be nourished. A baby seahorse is called a **fry**.

Predators and threats

Seahorses are on the menu for a lot of animals. Mostly larger fish including sharks, turtles and marine mammals ... and even people!

Seahorses can live for up to 10 years but, based on some large specimens which have been found, we think that they sometimes live for much longer.

Although listed as 'Least Concern', Pot-bellied Seahorses still face many threats from people. They are popular pets in the aquarium trade and are often illegally poached from the wild. Their habitat is mainly within coastal zones with water up to 100 metres deep. Because they live so close to the coast, their habitat has been adversely affected by humans.

How can we help seahorses?

I'm so glad that you asked!

Seagrass beds, coral reefs and even rocky outcrops are often polluted or destroyed by humans. Seahorse populations worldwide are vulnerable to overexploitation for medicinal and decorative purposes. There are no known health benefits from ingesting dried seahorse.

Next time you go on a family holiday, make sure you don't buy a souvenir made from seahorse.

SCAN HERE
to watch a WILD clip

txzyfq

Southern Blue-ringed Octopus

'When looks can kill.'

Hapalochlaena maculosa

Beware deadly venom! Blue-ringed octopus are infamous for being among the world's most venomous creatures. There are at least four species in the genus *Hapalochlaena*, and more scientific research is being conducted that could possibly discover even more. Australia's southern coastline is home to the Southern Blue-ringed Octopus.

Southern Blue-ringed Octopus feed mainly on crabs and other crustaceans. They inject the venom by biting and paralysing their prey. For smaller prey it is possible to release the venom into the water around them, which can also cause paralysis.

Classification

KINGDOM:	Animalia
PHYLUM:	Mollusca
CLASS:	Cephalopoda
ORDER:	Octopoda
FAMILY:	Octopodidae
GENUS:	*Hapalochlaena*
SPECIES:	*maculosa*

What's in a name?

Believe it or not, blue-ringed octopus are cousins to the humble terrestrial snails found in your garden – they both belong to the phylum **Mollusca**.

The order Octopoda refers to ancient Greek **octo** meaning 'eight' and **poda** meaning 'feet'.

Where is it found?

Several different species can be found around the coasts of Australia. They can also be found in the Indian and Pacific Oceans from Australia to Japan. The Southern Blue-ringed Octopus occurs along the southern coasts of Australia.

Blue-ringed octopus are found in habitats close to the shore at depths of up to 50 metres. They spend most of their time among rocky or reef-like structures in order to camouflage themselves and avoid predators.

Amazing adaptations and morphology

Southern Blue-ringed Octopus have a body around 5–6 centimetres long and eight arms of 10–11 centimetres. The arms are attached to each other by webbing which is extremely flexible and elastic. The large head is called a mantle and contains most vital internal organs including the gills, and **three hearts**. At the base of the mantle is the siphon, which is a tube-like muscle the octopus uses to push water through for movement and oxygenation.

Wow, they move around with jet propulsion!

They are often sandy to pale or dark brown in colour. The blue 'rings' aren't always visible, only appearing as a warning when the animal feels threatened. The blue-ringed octopus has two eyes and a beak located on the underside at the centre of its limbs. A bite from blue-ringed octopus can be fatal as the salivary glands in the octopus's mouth produce an extremely potent venom.

Eye

Mantle

Suckers

Siphon

Arms

Distinct blue rings

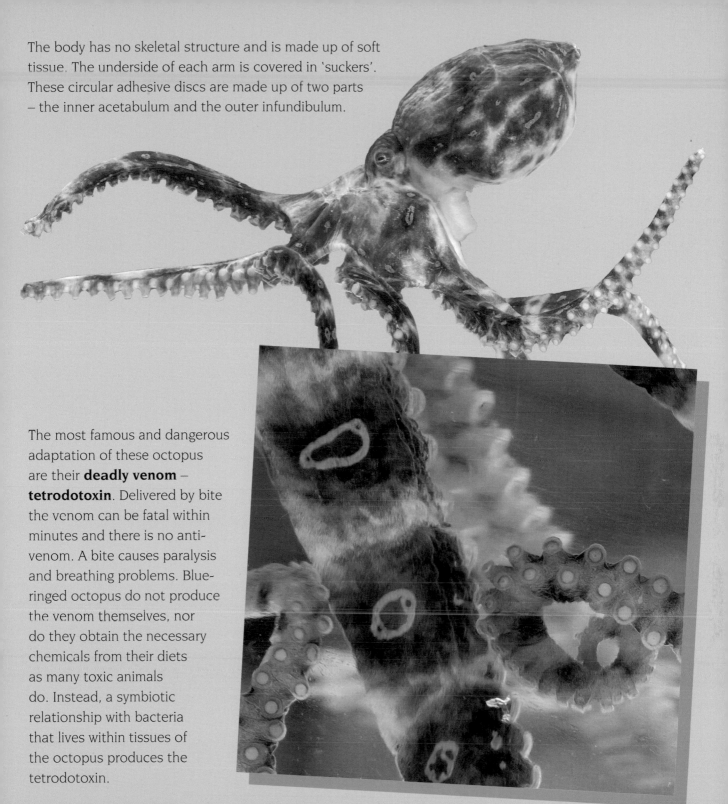

The body has no skeletal structure and is made up of soft tissue. The underside of each arm is covered in 'suckers'. These circular adhesive discs are made up of two parts – the inner acetabulum and the outer infundibulum.

The most famous and dangerous adaptation of these octopus are their **deadly venom – tetrodotoxin**. Delivered by bite the venom can be fatal within minutes and there is no anti-venom. A bite causes paralysis and breathing problems. Blue-ringed octopus do not produce the venom themselves, nor do they obtain the necessary chemicals from their diets as many toxic animals do. Instead, a symbiotic relationship with bacteria that lives within tissues of the octopus produces the tetrodotoxin.

The mouthpart of the blue-ringed octopus is the only hard part of its body. It is located at the base of the octopus's head, in the centre of its eight arms. The beak is made from **chitin**, a protein-based compound.

The lack of a skeletal structure is an adaptation that allows even large octopuses to squeeze their entire bodies through holes as small as 2–3 centimetres across. This ability enables them to hide in the smallest crevices to avoid predators.

The ability to change the colour of their skin is due to a special kind of cell called a **chromatophore**. These cells reflect light and contain pigments that allow them to change the colour of their skin, in this case to create blue rings to warn of their toxicity.

The bright blue warning colour is their way of saying 'back off, otherwise you'll pay the price.

Life cycle

The Southern Blue-ringed Octopus has a short lifespan of between 1 to 2 years. Both the male and female die shortly after they have fulfilled their reproductive duties.

The mating ritual begins with the male finding a female then caressing her with a specialised tentacle called the hectocotylus. This arm has been modified so it can deliver spermatophores to the female's oviduct, which is located under the mantle.

After mating the male dies while the female lays 50–100 eggs. The female will guard the eggs until they hatch without moving to eat. The eggs hatch within 50 days and the female dies shortly after from exhaustion and starvation.

The Southern Blue-ringed Octopus does not have a planktonic life stage after hatching. Instead, upon hatching the young are about the size of a pea and can begin feeding on pieces of crab within a week. The young octopus become mature in as little as four months.

Eggs

0–6 week hatchlings

6+ week hatchlings

Adult

Predators and threats

Despite their deadly venom blue-ringed octopus have a few predators, including sharks, eels and other fish, birds and seals.

Southern Blue-ringed Octopus populations haven't been extensively studied in the wild and it is assumed that they are stable. The greatest threat they may face from humans is through poaching from the wild for the aquarium trade, where they are a favourable species due to their inability to ink.

Because it favours coastal waters, this species could be affected by any human development in these areas, and by the pollution that is a by-product.

How can we help blue-ringed octopus?

Please ensure that you recycle all household litter and plastic waste, so it doesn't escape into storm water and out into our oceans.

Use biodegradable household products, which cause less harm to the environment.

When visiting the beach, always walk your dog on a lead, and if it decides to use the 'doggy-bathroom', pick up its poo. It is vital that we keep our beaches and intertidal rocky shores free from pollutants that detrimentally affect our amazing marine wildlife.

Look but don't touch! Enjoy rock pool rambling with family and friends. However, always spare a thought for our rockpool denizens. Please don't stress them out, admire them from afar, and marvel at their truly fascinating lives.

SCAN HERE
to watch a WILD clip

mplbqf

Great Spider Crab

Leptomithrax gaimardii

'I'm not a spider – I have ten legs.'

Famous for its mass aggregations in the winter months. Safety in numbers protects these crabs from predation when they have soft adult bodies after moulting their exoskeleton skin – this is when they are at their most vulnerable.

Although Great Spider Crabs are nimble and quite quick on their feet to chase down prey, mostly they tend to **scavenge** the sea floor for dead fish, molluscs, algae and even other crustaceans.

Great Spider Crabs are an extremely important organism in the mid trophic level of the food chain. They play a very important role consuming decaying matter and dead animals on the sea floor. And many predators gorge themselves on these vulnerable soft-bodied crabs after the have sloughed their skin.

They are like the garbage collectors of the ocean.

Classification

KINGDOM:	Animalia
PHYLUM:	Arthropoda
CLASS:	Malacostraca
ORDER:	Decapoda
FAMILY:	Majidae
GENUS:	*Leptomithrax*
SPECIES:	*gaimardii*

What's in a name?

Spider crabs, belong to the phylum Arthropoda, meaning that they have an exoskeleton, and jointed body parts and limbs.

The Great Spider Crab belongs to the class of Arthropods called the Malacostraca. **Malacos** is derived from the ancient Greek word for 'soft' and **ostrakon** means 'shell'.

The name of the order Decapoda is a dead giveaway that these creatures have ten legs!

The family name of the Great Spider Crab – Majidae – is derived from the Arabic word **majid**, which means 'noble, glorious, magnificent ... great!'

They are certainly great, as they are Victoria's largest spider crab.

The genus name L*eptomithrax* can be broken down in ancient Greek **lepto**, meaning 'slender', and **mithrax**, meaning 'gem' or 'opal'.

The species name *gaimardii*, is named in honour of French surgeon and naturalist Joseph Paul Gaimard.

Wouldn't it be super cool to have an animal species named in honour of yourself?

Don't forget, all crustaceans have two pairs of antennae!

Where is it found?

This species is found in coastal marine waters off south-eastern Australia, in a variety of habitats including sand, reef and among macro algae. They are more common in shallow water, however they have been found down to depths of 820 metres!

The Great Spider Crab is famous for congregating in thousands under jetties and in the shallow waters of Port Phillip Bay, Victoria, where they have become quite a tourist attraction.

Amazing adaptations and morphology

Masters of disguise, a spider crab's rough and spiny exoskeleton is a perfect real estate for algae, sponges and sea squirts to grow, enabling a spider crab to literally vanish into its habitat.

Now you see me, now you don't.

Each segmented spider-crab leg ends with a sharp point – a great adaptation for climbing and gripping onto rocks and the sea floor.

They are akin to the 'ice-picks' that mountaineers use for climbing and gripping. You wouldn't want a pinch from one of those things – OUCH!

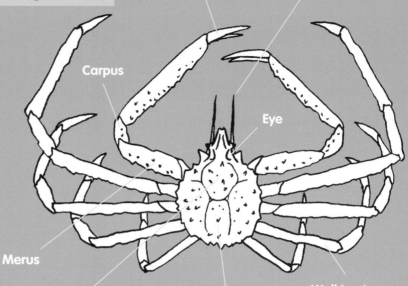

Claw or Chela

Antenna

Carpus

Eye

Merus

Cephalothorax

Abdomen

Walking legs

The Great Spider Crab is equipped with large pincers that are perfect for gripping and tearing their food. Spider crabs have been known to be **cannibalistic** and eat their own kind!

The hard exoskeleton affords the spider crab protection from predators and the turbulent environment of the southern seas.

It's a bit like people wearing a bicycle helmet for protection.

Amazingly, if a spider crab loses a leg from an attack by a predator, it can regrow the limb next time it moults its skin. There is a special 'weakness plane' across the leg. When a predator grabs the crab's leg, the muscles contract to pinch off the nerves and prevent loss of fluid. However, it may take up to six sheddings of the skin before the limb fully grows back.

It was once thought that the mass gatherings of spider crabs in winter was a sign of breeding behaviour. Now, scientists are more inclined to believe that it is a safety-in-numbers strategy. The winter moult of their exoskeleton leaves them vulnerable. It can take two hours for a crab to shed its exoskeleton, then re-expand and hydrate its body, and finally harden the new exoskeleton. During this period, it is easy prey for predators.

Spider crabs are crustaceans. They have two pairs of antennae and two body segments. The head and body are fused together to make the **cephalothorax**. The abdomen is underneath the main body.

Did you know that an aggregation of crabs is called a CAST?

The Great Spider Crab has a carapace which is longer than it is wide, so superficially the crab resembles an arachnid.

Under a microscope the Great Spider Crab's exoskeleton is covered with tiny hooks. These are a perfect growing medium to collect and snag small pieces of sponge and algae species."

That's like Velcro – the spider crab is a moving garden of living organisms!

Life cycle

Like many other crabs, Great Spider Crabs have a very interesting life cycle. After mating, the female protects the fertilised eggs under her big round abdomen. The eggs hatch as tiny larvae called **zoea**, which swim and grow in the plankton 'soup' of the ocean until they are large enough to establish themselves on the seafloor as miniature crabs and grow!

Great Spider Crabs grow in distinct stages. Each time a crab moults its old protective shell it exposes its soft shell, which then hardens at a new bigger size.

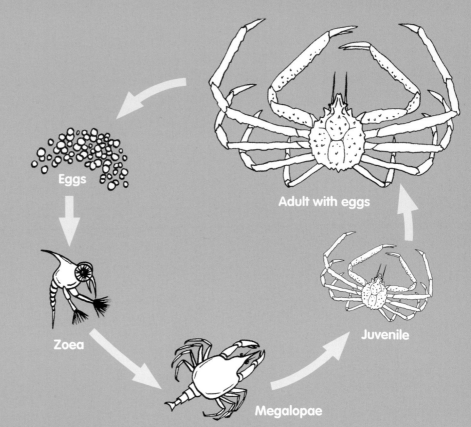

Eggs

Zoea

Megalopae

Juvenile

Adult with eggs

"Hey that beats having to spend money on new clothes at the shops!"

Predators and threats

Rays, sharks and other fish, as well as seabirds, seals and dolphins, relish a great feast when spider crabs gather en masse to moult their skin.

People fish and collect Great Spider Crabs. A bag limit of 15 animals may be taken by an individual in any one day, although these crabs are not renowned for their edibility!

The great congregations are a true marvel of nature and attracts divers and sightseers.

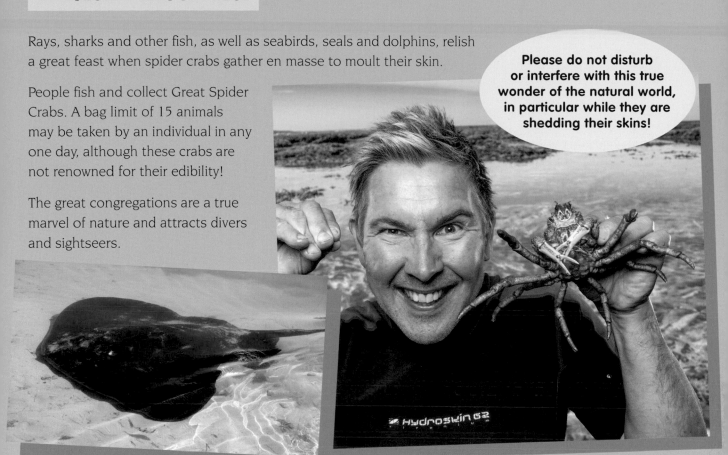

Please do not disturb or interfere with this true wonder of the natural world, in particular while they are shedding their skins!

How can we help Great Spider Crabs?

Little is known about the lives of these crabs after they depart from their mass gatherings and head into deeper waters. Mass gatherings cannot be predicted, and vary in size, densities and timings every year in Australia's southern waters. People are encouraged to report sightings of Great Spider Crab congregations via a citizen science app run by Deakin University. It is hoped that scientists can piece together the data collected from the general public, to learn more about this fascinating crustacean.

What a great idea – I'm going to download the app today.

SCAN HERE
to watch a WILD clip

tumaso

Port Jackson Shark

Heterodontus portusjacksoni

'The most amazing egg that you'll ever see.'

What's in a name?

Port Jackson Shark belongs to the class Chondrichthyes and is a cartilaginous fish. Sharks, rays and skates all belong to this class.

The species name refers to Port Jackson in New South Wales, where this species is commonly observed.

The Port Jackson shark belongs to the order **Heterodontiformes**. In ancient Greek **hetero** means 'different' and **odont** means 'teeth'. This refers to the two different types of teeth they have in their mouth – incisors for grabbing and molars for crushing and grinding. The anterior teeth are small and pointed, whereas the posterior teeth are broad and flat.

The teeth function to hold and break, then crush and grind the shells of molluscs and echinoderms. Juvenile Port Jackson Sharks have more pointed teeth and feed on a higher proportion of soft-bodied prey than adults.

They are sometimes called horn sharks, bullheads and tabbigaws, as well as pigfish!

Where is it found?

They live on or near the bottom of the ocean to depths of 250m. They prefer rocky, sandy, coral or sea-grass habitats.

Port Jackson Sharks are endemic to the waters surrounding the southern half of Australia.

'Endemic' means that they are found nowhere else.

Amazing morphology and adaptations

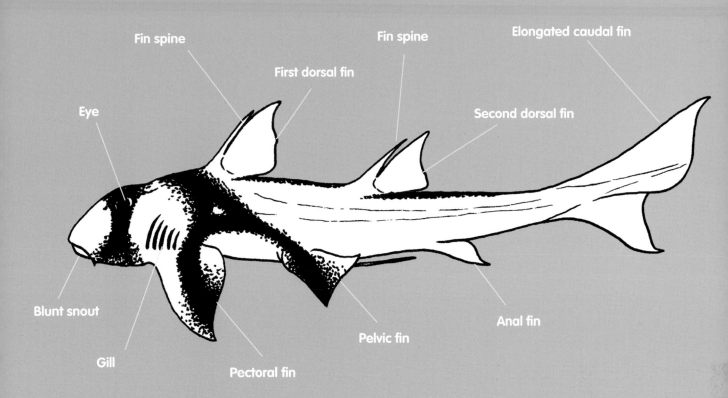

Fin spine

Fin spine

Elongated caudal fin

First dorsal fin

Eye

Second dorsal fin

Blunt snout

Anal fin

Gill

Pelvic fin

Pectoral fin

These sharks can grow up to 1.65 metres in length and typically the females are larger than the males. They are a pale grey-brown colour with darker markings around the eyes and along the body.

The skin is made up of millions of microscopic scales called **denticles**. They make the shark's skin feel very rough and very tough.

The skin feels like dad's face in the morning before he has a shave. It's as rough as sandpaper!

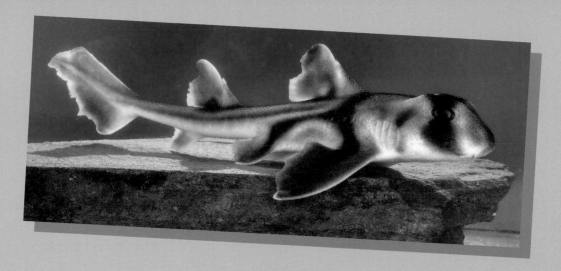

They have a raised ridge above the eyes and two dorsal fins with spines on the leading edge that can be used to protect them from predators. In juveniles the spines are quite sharp, but they become more blunt with age.

Port Jackson Sharks have five gill slits, a pair each of pectoral fins and pelvic fins, and a single anal fin. The tail fin, also called a caudal fin, is elongated.

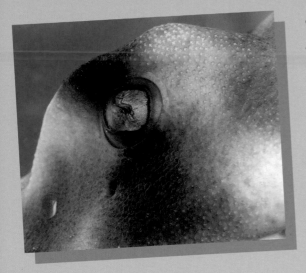

The banded patterns across their body help them to blend in against the sea floor. Port Jackson Sharks commonly have a dark band across their eyes and, starting from the first dorsal fin, a harness-shaped pattern across the back.

Port Jackson Sharks differ from other sharks because of their ability to eat and breathe at the same time. The first gill is enlarged and can pump water across the other four even while they stay still.

These sharks are **nocturnal** to make sure they are awake when their prey is! They eat an assortment of molluscs, echinoderms, crustaceans and fish.

Some of their food is very spiny, and if a sea urchin isn't digesting well the shark can turn its stomach inside-out, emptying the offending contents through its mouth before pulling the stomach back inside.

Wow!
Fancy being able to spit your stomach out of your mouth. Gross!

They look like they are wearing a Zorro mask and a dog harness!

Life cycle

The breeding season for Port Jackson Sharks is late winter to early spring, or August to November. These sharks are oviparous, meaning that the females are egg layers. They begin laying eggs from October. The eggs are soft and double-helix spiral-shaped to help lodge them into crevices and reefs where they then harden.

The eggs are laid in pairs and the females can lay eggs every two weeks, laying 10–16 by the end of the breeding season.

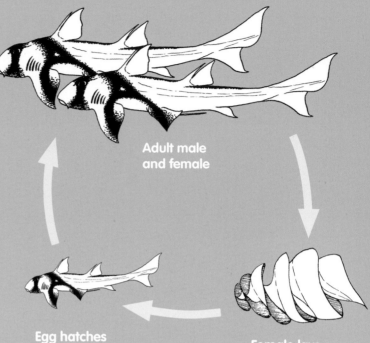

Adult male and female

Female lays egg

Egg hatches

The unique shape of the egg case is an excellent adaptation for a shark that lays around on reefs and rocky outcrops. When the egg is first laid it is soft and pliable. The female picks it up with her mouth and pushes it into a crevice or coral. As the egg hardens it becomes stuck to the area where the female placed it.

Perfect for wedging into rocks on the ocean floor – safe from hungry predators and strong currents.

The eggs won't hatch for another 10–12 months. The young sharks, called pups, are only 20–30 centimetres in length when they hatch. Pups are likely to stay close to bays and estuaries until they reach maturity, which is at around 8–10 years for males and 11–14 years for females. Port Jackson Sharks are believed to live for up to 30 years.

Next time you go for a walk along the beach, keep an eye out for the washed-up empty egg cases of Port Jackson Sharks.

Predators and threats

Not a lot is known about the predators of Port Jackson Sharks, although we do know that juveniles and unhatched eggs are more likely to end up as a meal. In fact, more than 80 per cent of developing embryos suffer mortality. Scientists believe that adults can fall prey to larger shark species such as Great White Sharks and Broad-nosed Seven-gilled Sharks.

Currently Port Jackson Sharks have a stable population, however because it takes roughly 10 years for juveniles to reach reproductive maturity, it could be many years before declines in populations are noticed. These sharks are often caught as by-catch in nets. Anglers often view them as pests and kill them before throwing back into the ocean.

Woah, that's appalling behaviour. What has the poor shark done to anyone? That is disgraceful.

SCAN HERE
to watch a WILD clip

zpcuns

Little Penguin

Eudyptula minor

'The world's smallest penguin.'

This is the world's smallest penguin species, growing to a pint-sized 35 centimetres in height and weighing around 1 kilogram. Compare this with the world's largest penguin, the Emperor Penguin, which grows to a height of 110 centimetres and 'weighs in' at 35 kilograms.

Despite the 'cuteness-overload' appearance, Little Penguins are important oceanic predators, keeping the balance in our natural world. Penguins are also a vital part of the food web, providing a source of food for many other ocean predators.

Did you know that MOST scientists concur that there are 18 different penguin species in the world. The Little Penguin is the smallest.

What's in a name?

The common name **penguin** comes from the Latin word **pinguis**, meaning 'fat'!

Penguins are differentiated from other birds in the class Aves, by being placed in the order Sphenisciformes, which literally breaks down into **phenesci**, which is Latin for 'wedge', and **formes**, which means 'shape' or 'form'.

The Little Penguin's binomial name **Eudyptula minor** translates to 'great little diver!'

This species has a few general common names. When I was a child, we called them Fairy Penguins. The species is also known as Little Blue Penguin and Blue Penguin.

Contrary to popular belief, unlike in the movie *Happy Feet*, not all penguins need to live on ice. Little Penguins are known as a temperate-climate species and do not need freezing Antarctic conditions to survive.

Classification

KINGDOM: Animalia
PHYLUM: Chordata
CLASS: Aves
ORDER: Sphenisciformes
FAMILY: Spheniscidae
GENUS: *Eudyptula*
SPECIES: *minor*

They can tolerate wide temperature extremes, from surviving swimming in the bitterly cold southern seas, to coping with extreme summer heat while raising their family on mainland southern Australia. Little Penguins seek shelter in their cooler burrows, where sometimes the external daytime temperature will reach 40°C.

Where is it found?

You won't find a Little Penguin living among the glaciers in Antarctica. Instead, they are found in marine waters around southern Australia, as well as around New Zealand.

Little Penguins breed on coasts from Fremantle, Western Australia, right along the southern coastline of Australia as far as Sydney, New South Wales, as well as around Tasmania. They prefer coastal rocky outcrops, which afford them burrowing sites to nest and places to shelter and avoid predation.

Amazing morphology and adaptations

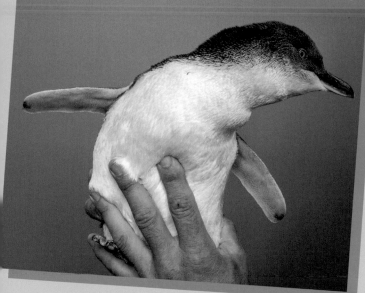

Their rather 'dapper' blue-and-white tuxedo pattern offers them camouflage in their watery world. The blue back helps them to avoid detection from above by potential aerial predators such as White-bellied Sea Eagles and large gulls, while the white belly helps to camouflage them against the sky when viewed from below by stealthy Killer Whales, fur seals and sharks that might be hunting swimming penguins.

Little Penguins can be rather dirty and messy in their land living quarters. To compensate for their rather shoddy housekeeping skills, they have the remarkable ability to projectile 'poo' up to a metre away, usually aiming away from the entrance of their burrow!

Did you know that penguins poop every 20 minutes or so? They have a very fast metabolism!

The sharp little hook at the tip of their beak is ideal for catching small pilchards, anchovies and squid.

It's like an in-built fishing hook – perfect for fishing.

Beak

Eye

Dark blue feathers on top

White feathers on belly

Flippers

Webbed feet

Claws

As well as a sharp and powerful beak for holding on to prey, these penguins have a **spiked tongue** to assist them in swallowing prey as they propel themselves through the water.

Little Penguins are perfectly adapted for surviving in the sometimes bitterly cold waters off southern Australia. Their dense protective layer of up to **10,000 small downy feathers** helps insulate their bodies. The feather density is three to four times that of their avian cousins who spend their lives on land.

The base of the penguin's feathers are very downy and soft, trapping air and creating an **insulating barrier** to protect the bird from the cold water. The tips of their feathers are harder and spear shaped, not unlike fish scales – these stop the water pressure from squeezing out the warm air trapped in the insulated layer.

It's like wearing a wet suit when you go swimming.

In the summer season, adult penguins gorge themselves on food to almost double their weight before they come to shore and moult. As Little Penguins spend 80 per cent of their lives in the sea, it is vital to ensure that damaged and worn feathers are replaced. During this moulting process, they lose all of their 10,000 feathers. This is known as a **catastrophic moult**. This process takes up to 17 days. During this period, the penguins do not venture out to sea or eat.

Penguins have a third transparent eyelid that slides across and helps them to see beneath the water. This is known as a **nictitating membrane**, and it's like a windscreen wiper to keep sand and other debris from their eyes.

Little Penguins' feet are short and stocky, perfect for rock hopping up cliffs and steep inclines. Their feet are webbed for swimming and also equipped with sharp claws to give extra grip on slippery, muddy surfaces.

A penguin's vision needs to be exceptional as they rely on it to locate and capture their prey. They even have in-built night vision.

Little Penguins have a **uropygial gland** located at the base of their tail feathers. This special gland secretes an oil which the penguin uses to **waterproof** itself.

Amazingly, Little Penguins have the 'super-nifty' ability to drink saline seawater.

Above the eyes they have a **supraorbital gland**, which helps to filter out all the salt ingested through drinking seawater.

Although Little Penguins can't take to the air and fly, they certainly do a brilliant job of flying through their watery home. They can reach a swimming speed of up to 6 kilometres per hour and have been recorded travelling 50 kilometres in one day. They spend most of their lives out at sea and can be away from land for up to four months at a time.

Life cycle

The Little Penguin's breeding season can stretch from August to February. In a single season these penguins are **monogamous**, which means that they have only one breeding partner. However, some individuals may find a new mate the following breeding season.

Both the male and female penguin help to gather material and prepare the nest. The female lays 1–2 eggs and both parents share in the incubation duties.

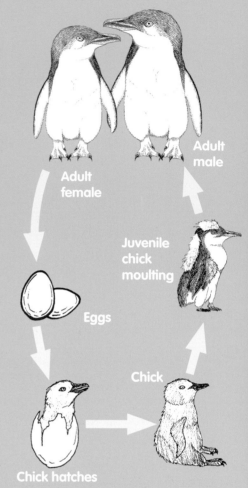

Adult male

Adult female

Juvenile chick moulting

Eggs

The eggs take 33–37 days to incubate and hatch. The chick has a special 'egg-tooth' on the upper tip of its beak, which it uses to chip its way out of the egg. Once a chick has 'pipped' the egg it can take up to three days to fully emerge, sometimes with little help from its parents. What a marathon!

Chick

Chick hatches

Penguin chicks are **semi-altricial** as they still require the nurturing and help from their parents for protection and food. Each parent takes turns with brooding duties, while the other one swims out to sea to hunt for food.

The chicks are covered in fluffy dark grey down when hatched. Their 'dapper' blue-and-white feathers start to emerge at four weeks of age.

There is nothing more adorable than a baby Little Penguin!

At this time the chicks are left alone in their burrow while both parents hunt at sea. At 8–9 weeks the young penguins make their first trips out to sea and become fully independent.

The average lifespan of a Little Penguin in the wild is seven years. However, a captive bird has been recorded living to the ripe old age of 21 years!

Predators and threats

The delightful and endearing Little Penguin faces so many threats to its survival. In the ocean they have many predators, such as seals, sharks and Killer Whales. While nesting and resting on land they aren't any safer – hungry goannas, sea eagles, snakes and introduced predators such as dogs, cats and foxes can all prove deadly. Even introduced rats can destroy eggs and kill young chicks.

Pollution and human waste have an overwhelmingly negative impact on Little Penguin populations. Penguins can easily become entangled in plastic waste and drown, they have also been known to consume plastic waste and die.

Oil spills, pollution, overfishing and destruction of nesting habitats due to human activity have all compounded the continued reduction in the population of the world's smallest penguin.

How can we help Little Penguins?

I'm so glad that you asked!

Please ensure that you recycle all household litter and plastic waste, so it doesn't escape into storm water and out into our oceans.

When visiting the beach, always walk your dog on a lead, so it doesn't run off and scare and eat native wildlife.

We can help Little Penguins by picking up rubbish and being responsible pet owners.

If you are lucky enough to see a wild Little Penguin, please don't disturb it. Remember, it is illegal to approach and interact with native wildlife. Severe penalties may apply.

Please don't use flash photography, as the light from your flash will frighten a penguin and can blind it for up to five minutes.

Always keep control of your pets, especially dogs. If you own a pet cat, please ensure that it is enclosed day and night in a pet enclosure. Both domestic and feral cats are devastating predators of the enigmatic Little Penguin.

Let's save them together for future generations.

SCAN HERE
to watch a WILD clip

yukjyw

Waratah Anemone

Actinia tenebrosa

'Hard to say, and even harder to spell.'

Sea anemones are susceptible to pollution and siltation, making them very important **environmental indicators**.

Their presence tells us that we live in a healthy place.

Waratah Anemones consume small shrimp, fish, worms and plankton. They are 'sit-and-wait' ambush specialists, stinging unsuspecting prey with their tentacles until the animal is subdued.

Woah, that's a gruesome way to die!

KINGDOM: Animalia
PHYLUM: Cnidaria
CLASS: Anthozoa
ORDER: Actinaria
FAMILY: Actiniidae
GENUS: *Actinia*
SPECIES: *tenebrosa*

What's in a name?

The phylum name **Cnidaria** comes from the Greek word for 'sea nettle', in reference to this animal's nematocysts, which are used for stinging and catching prey.

The word **Anthozoa** is derived from the ancient Greek word meaning 'flower animal'.

The genus name is *Actinia*. In ancient Greek **Actin** means 'filament' or 'rays' and here it refers to the mass of tiny stinging tentacles that trap the anemone's prey. The species name ***tenebrosa*** means 'dark and gloomy' in Greek.

It certainly looks like the New South Wales floral emblem, the red waratah flower.

This animal is also sometimes called a **cherry anemone** because of its deep red velvety colour.

Where is it found?

Cnidarians are some of the most common inhabitants in cooler intertidal waters. They are usually found on hard rocky substrates.

The Waratah Anemone is the most noticeable anemone along the rocky coastlines of southern Australia and New Zealand, living in rockpools up to a depth of 5 metres. It prefers to live in rocky crevices and under ledges.

At low tide it contracts itself to avoid desiccation.

They remind me of an upturned 'wobbly' red jelly! But make sure that you hang around for the tide to come back in – that's when the Waratah Anemone shows off its true colours.

Amazing adaptations and morphology

Waratah Anemones do not have a brain, but they do have a nervous system. The body of a sea anemone is called a **column**.

Sea anemones are **radially symmetrical**, with the mouth positioned directly in the middle, allowing the animal to detect prey and predators from all directions.

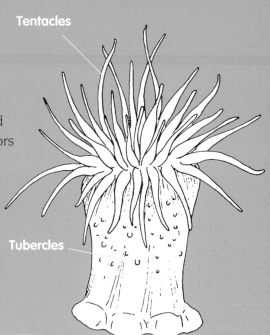

Tentacles

Tubercles

Basal disc

The Waratah Anemone attaches itself to hard surfaces with a **basal disc**.

That's like a big suction cup – they are impossible to move once stuck.

Waratah Anemones can move, albeit at a 'snail's pace'. An anemone can detach the basal disc and slowly move to a favourable site.

Living in in the intertidal zone, anemones are subject to extremely hostile environmental conditions with abrupt changes. As the tide recedes, they show amazing behaviour by 'shutting up shop'. With the lower water pressure, they contract their tentacles into the mouth and halve their size, minimising exposure to the air. As the high tide returns, the anemone increases its water pressure and bursts back to full 'flower'.

Waratah Anemone tentacles are arranged in three **whorls** which sprout out from the **acontia**. An individual can be armed with up to 200 red **tentacles** that are responsible for feeding. They are armed with hundreds of tiny stinging nematocyst cells for immobilising and catching prey. Once captured the tentacles are responsible for moving prey towards the mouth.

Sea anemones maintain water pressure equilibrium using syphons. One syphon draws in water while the other siphon pumps it out.

Did you know that the Waratah Anemone is harmless to touch and is unlikely to sting a person.

Did you know that an anemone's mouth is also its bottom?!

Life cycle

Incredibly the Waratah Anemone reproduces both sexually and asexually. **Sexual reproduction** involves broadcast spawning resulting in larvae joining the ocean's plankton soup; these eventually settle on rocks far away from the parents. **Asexual reproduction** allows the young to brood and develop inside the safety of the coelenteron. When fully developed the larvae are ejected and spewed out from the parent's tentacle-lined mouth. The baby anemones then stick to a rock surface close to the parent, creating a cluster of related anemones. Disgusting but cool – an anemone creche!

Adult

Fertilised egg

Planula

Polyp

Young anemone polyp

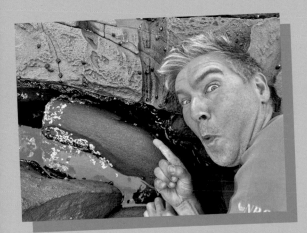

The larvae often settle close to the parent animal, forming a colony of related Waratah Anemones. Larvae can also drift pelagically and settle, colonising new territories and habitats.

Wow, they give birth to live young just like people do.

The Waratah Anemone can also reproduce asexually and can clone itself.

So theoretically an anemone could live forever if it were free from predation and pollution.

Predators and threats

The Waratah Anemone has very few natural predators. However, the Grey Side-gilled Slug has a penchant for gobbling them up.

People can have a deleterious effect on Waratah Anemone populations. Coastal development can increase pollution and solids in the intertidal zone, disturbing the feeding habits and health of these animals.

Climate change is a huge pressure on the Waratah Anemone. Rising seawater temperatures will affect anemone abundance, and likely lead to the species' range shrinking southwards.

Continued ocean acidification will likely affect body condition and breeding success, making Waratah Anemones more susceptible to disease and predation.

How can we help sea anemones?

We can all do our part in protecting our rocky shores. Why not become a citizen scientist and record your observations next time you visit the intertidal zone. There are many organisations and groups you can join. It's heaps of fun and your observations will help document changes in sea anemone populations and the overall health of the environment.

Slender-spined Porcupinefish

Diodon nicthemerus

'Toxic flesh, beware – eat me if you dare!'

Classification

KINGDOM:	Animalia
PHYLUM:	Chordata
CLASS:	Actinopterygii
ORDER:	Tetraodontiformes
FAMILY:	Diodontidae
GENUS:	*Diodon*
SPECIES:	*nicthemerus*

What's in a name?

These fish are also commonly known as **pufferfish**, **globefish** or **blowfish**, with these names describing its ability to 'puff-up' when provoked or agitated.

The genus name **Diodon** refers to the fact that they practically only have two teeth – **dio** means 'two' and **odonto** means 'teeth'. The porcupinefish teeth form a powerful beak, which is perfect for grazing and collecting food.

> **It's almost like a pair of pliers in a toolbox.**

The scientific species name **nicthemerus** translates into English as 'night and day', describing the predominantly nocturnal feeding behaviour of this prickly fish and its more sedentary reclusive nature during the daytime, when it tends to seek shelter among sea algae and rocky crags.

This is one of the smallest members in the porcupinefish family, growing to a maximum size of 28 centimetres. However, on average most grow to about half that length.

Where is it found?

This porcupinefish is found in marine waters off southern Australia from Port Jackson, New South Wales, around to Geraldton, Western Australia. It is also found off Tasmania, usually in shallow coastal waters and inlets. It is very common in Port Phillip Bay, Victoria.

It prefers to live in rocky, sandy, grassy flats, and can be often seen beneath jetties. Juveniles are pelagic and can gather in large numbers near the surface in open water, usually seeking refuge in drifting macro algae.

It could be described as a football with a tail.

Amazing adaptations and morphology

The nocturnal porcupinefish has huge 'boggle' eyes, which are perfect for night vision. They are generally more active at night, only venturing out in daytime during low light levels, for example when it is overcast. In the day, porcupinefish lurk around in macro algae or beneath jetties and other structures.

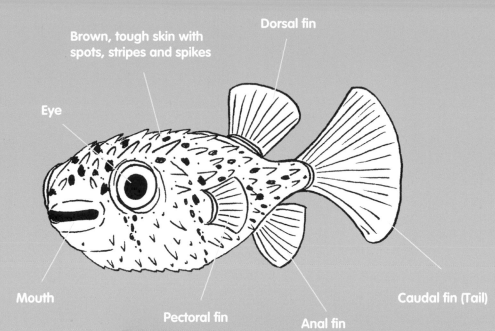

Brown, tough skin with spots, stripes and spikes

Dorsal fin

Eye

Mouth

Pectoral fin

Anal fin

Caudal fin (Tail)

The Slender-spined Porcupinefish has a robust body shape but has the ability to move quickly if needed.

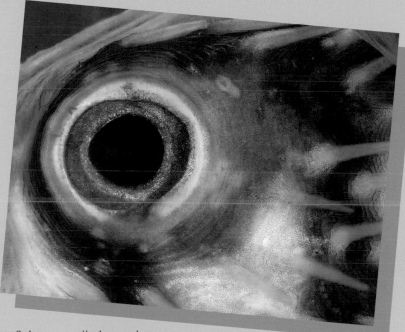

These porcupinefishes usually have three to four darker bands or blotches on their bodies, which help them to expertly camouflage themselves in their 'watery' world.

107

Their teeth are shaped like a beak and grow continuously. They are extremely sharp and their jaws very powerful. These fish feed on an array of benthic invertebrates, such as shrimps, crabs, sea urchins and mussels, using the strong beak to crush prey effortlessly.

When danger is afoot, the porcupinefish are quick to defend themselves by rapidly inflating their bodies with air or water.

A porcupinefish body is covered in modified scales with usually white or yellow spines bent towards the tail. When the fish is threatened these erect, offering instant protection.

Divers have had their fingers bitten off by this seemingly friendly-looking fish.

OUCH, you certainly would think twice about eating a porcupinefish – you'd get prickles caught in your mouth.

These dense spines send a clear message to any would-be attacker – if eaten, a porcupinefish could easily become wedged in the throat of a predator.

The impressive threat display and bright yellow colours may also remind predators of their lethal skin, which contains a substance called **tetrodotoxin**. This has molecules 1,200 times more toxic than cyanide. Tetrodotoxin is the same toxin found in a blue-ringed octopus's venom.

The flesh of porcupinefish and their close cousins the toadfish are highly poisonous if ingested by humans, and they have been responsible for several deaths in Australia.

Did you know that Captain Cook's second voyage was almost cut short when he visited New Caledonia and ate the flesh of a pufferfish?

WARNING:
Cooking the meat of this species does not deactivate the poison.
If a person eats a large quantity of flesh, death could result in less than two hours.

That's why these fish appear to have a BIG smile on their face – they know they have plenty of tricks in their bag.

Life cycle

Slender-spined Porcupinefish are **broadcast spawners**. When breeding, the male and female swim near the surface of the water and release their reproductive cells. Once fused together the fertilised eggs are abandoned and left to drift on ocean currents.

The eggs incubate over a very short period of five days or so. Upon hatching the young **fry** are well developed, exhibiting eyes, a mouth and a swim bladder.

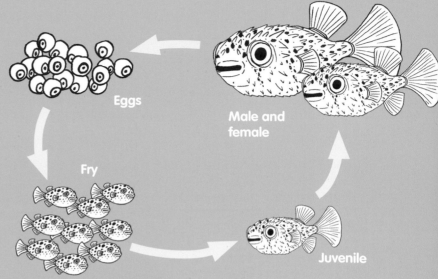

Eggs

Male and female

Fry

Juvenile

The young drift in the ocean currents gaining nourishment from pelagic plankton. After increasing in size they migrate back to shallow waters and grow into adults.

Predators and threats

Very few predators are game enough to eat these fish, but unfortunately, because of their spines and their habitats, they often become **by-catch** victims in scallop nets.

Worldwide, the porcupinefish (or pufferfish) is collected for the aquarium trade and for tourist souvenirs. **Overcollection** is a risk to many species in the wild.

When porcupinefish become stressed, alarmed or frightened they will puff out.

The only known predator of adult porcupinefish of any species is the Tiger Shark. However, the pelagic juveniles fall victim to a myriad of predators.

Thankfully, due to Slender-spined Porcupinefish being prolific spawners, the species is not considered to be threatened.

Pufferfish are used for the potentially deadly Japanese meal called **fugu**. This famed delicacy is prepared by well-trained experienced chefs, who remove the toxic organs from the fish.

How can we help Slender-spined Porcupinefish?

If caught on a fishing line, release the fish back into the ocean. Please don't be cruel and force the porcupinefish to blow up with air, as this is stressful on the fish and the animal will suffocate out of the water.

Southern Biscuit Seastar

Tosia australis

'It looks more like a colourful biscuit from the bakery than an animal!'

This diminutive seastar is heavily armour-plated, as it lives in highly volatile intertidal environments where the waves crash and bash it onto rocky seashores!

Southern Biscuit Seastars are omnivorous, feasting on sponges, cunjevoi, bryozoans and algae.

The common name of this pretty echinoderm makes perfect sense; it looks like it came from a cookie jar!

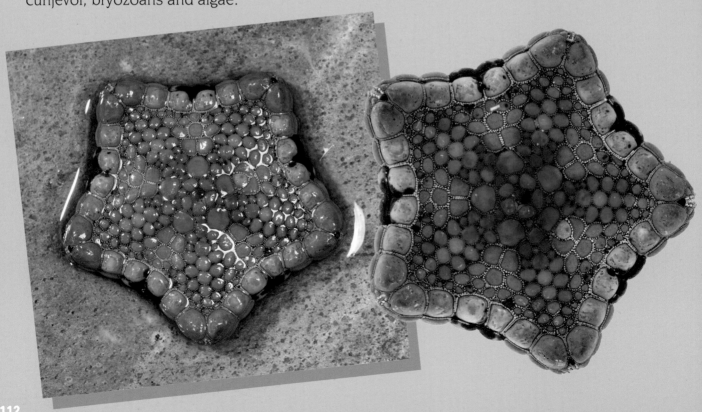

Classification

KINGDOM: Animalia
PHYLUM: Echinodermata
CLASS: Asteroidea
ORDER: Valvatida
FAMILY: Goniasteridae
GENUS: *Tosia*
SPECIES: *australis*

What's in a name?

The genus name **Tosia** is intriguing, as it is derived from an ancient Greek girl's name, meaning 'bold, pioneering and determined'. What an apt name for this small and plucky little seastar, which lives in one of the most inhospitable environments in the world – Australia's southern coastline.

The species name **australis** refers to its distribution, as it is endemic to southern Australian coastal waters.

Biscuit seastars belong to the class **Asteroidea**, which in ancient Greek means 'star-like'.

Where is it found?

Common along the rocky shores of New South Wales, Victoria, South Australia, Western Australia and Tasmania, occurring down to depths of 40 metres.

Amazing adaptations and morphology

Protected by large **plates** on each side of its body, the Southern Biscuit Seastar is well adapted for survival in the rocky intertidal zone. Amazingly, seastars which live in more exposed ocean environments have more bulbous plates on the ends of their arms! This seastar has six (rarely eight) plates along the edge between each arm tip.

This firm-bodied seastar is covered with a mosaic of tessellated plates which offer further protection from rough seas, where the animal may be dislodged or thrown about. They also afford protection from predators.

The body is a hard, flat, disc-like structure

Different colours, textures and patterns to help camouflage

Eye spot

Tubular feet

Mouth

It sure is one tough little customer – that's like bumper bars on a dodgem car.

Seastars have their mouth on the underside, so they are perfectly adapted for grazing as they move across rocky reefs.

Seastars move about using **tube feet**. Each hydrostatic foot is comprised of a sucker called an **ampulla** and a **podium**. When a seastar needs to create suction at the end of the tube feet, the ampullae pull water out of the podia, creating suction. A seastar appears to be floating as it moves about the intertidal zone, with hundreds of tube feet working simultaneously to propel it forwards.

At the end of each tube foot there is a set of cells which exude a seastar 'super glue' that helps them to grip and move about. One cell exudes the glue, and the cell next to it has a chemical which dissolves the glue. Seastars are known to leave a trail behind them.

WOW, seastars leave footprints!

The biscuit seastar's tube feet are protected by **ambulacral grooves** which extend from the mouth to the end of the arm. These grooves can be tightened and closed, protecting the seastar from potentially drying out if stranded above the water line at low tide.

That's a very clever way to hold your breath.

If you closely observe a biscuit seastar it has an opening called a **madreporite** on the top part of its body. Water is drawn in and travels through the body using a vascular network of tubes.

WOW, seastars don't have blood like humans do. Instead, seawater is pumped through the body to assist in locomotion as well as being a source of nutrients and gas exchange.

Perhaps the sometimes garish colours of a biscuit seastar help to protect it from attack by would-be predators. Bright colours often act as a deterrent as they could be deemed toxic or distasteful.

Growing to only 5 centimetres across, this seastar's petite size and flattened shape enable it to hide expertly in secluded and protected fissures in rocks along the southern Australian intertidal zone.

The biscuit seastar has five distinct arms – this is known as **pentameral symmetry**.

Life cycle

Like most seastars, biscuit seastars can reproduce in two ways. A male and female can release their reproductive cells into the ocean, the eggs become fertilised and the larval seastars drift around in pelagic currents until they get bigger and descend to the ocean floor to grow into adult seastars.

Alternatively, seastars can reproduce by **fission**. Remarkably, they have ability to **clone** themselves – they literally break in half to create an exact replica.

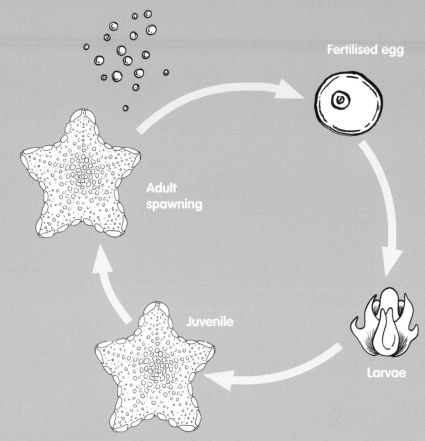

Fertilised egg

Adult spawning

Juvenile

Larvae

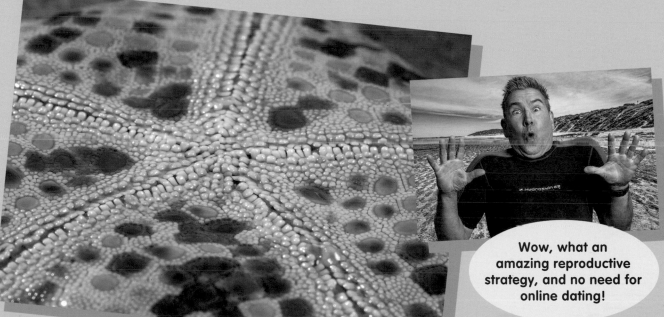

Wow, what an amazing reproductive strategy, and no need for online dating!

117

Predators and threats

Seabirds such as gulls, shorebirds such as oystercatchers, benthic-feeding fish and rays would all dine on a biscuit seastar if given the opportunity.

Habitat loss and degradation are also increasing threats for this colourful ocean denizen.

The biggest threat to biscuit seastars in the intertidal zone is polluted run-off caused by people.

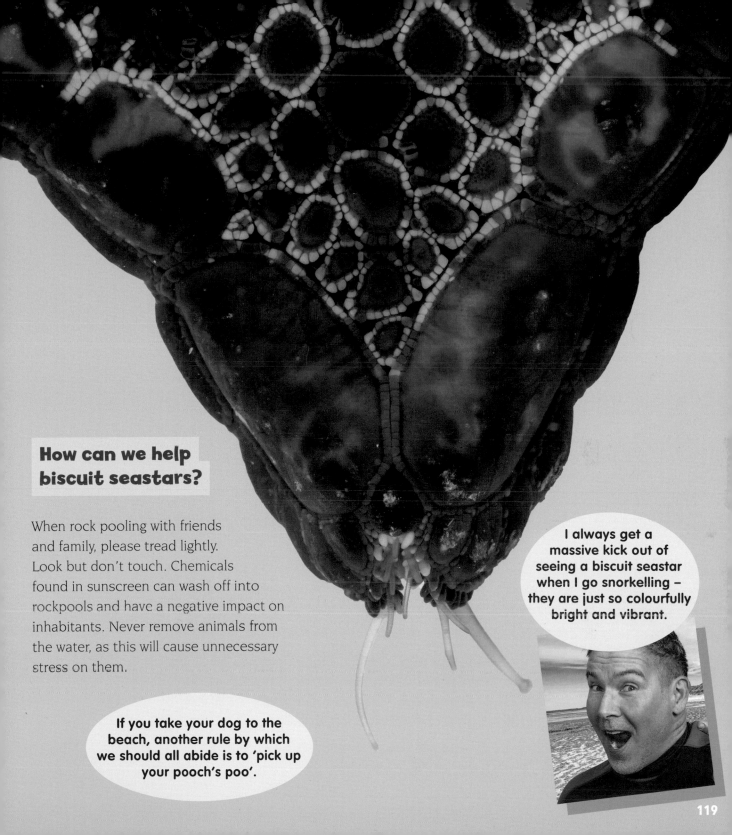

How can we help biscuit seastars?

When rock pooling with friends and family, please tread lightly. Look but don't touch. Chemicals found in sunscreen can wash off into rockpools and have a negative impact on inhabitants. Never remove animals from the water, as this will cause unnecessary stress on them.

If you take your dog to the beach, another rule by which we should all abide is to 'pick up your pooch's poo'.

I always get a massive kick out of seeing a biscuit seastar when I go snorkelling – they are just so colourfully bright and vibrant.

119

Weedy Seadragon

Phyllopteryx taeniolatus

'Victoria's state marine emblem, and a master of disguise.'

Weedy Seadragons are an important mid-trophic predator of Australia's southern rocky shorelines. They themselves are predated upon by larger animals, so they are an important part of a healthy **food web** and ecosystem.

Their mystical appearance, incredible colours and bizarre reproductive biology make them a 'standout' for a Victoria's state marine emblem.

I remember the first time a saw a Weedy Seadragon in the wild – it was absolutely breathtaking. This is my all-time favourite fish.

Classification

KINGDOM: Animalia
PHYLUM: Chordata
CLASS: Actinopterygii
ORDER: Sygnathiformes
FAMILY: Sygnathidae
GENUS: *Phyllopteryx*
SPECIES: *taeniolatus*

What's in a name?

The genus name **Phyllopteryx** can be broken down into ancient Greek **phyllon** meaning 'leaf' and **pteryx** meaning 'wing'.

The species name **taeniolatus** is derived from the Latin word meaning 'ribbon' or 'banded'.

This spectacular fish is a close relative of the seahorses.

Where is it found?

Growing to about 30–45 centimetres in length, the Weedy Seadragon is found in the intertidal zone to depths of 50 metres. It is found only in Australia, along rocky coastlines from Geraldton in Western Australia, through South Australia, Victoria and Tasmania, to Port Stephens in New South Wales.

These seadragons live in waters with temperatures between 12–23°C, favouring rocky reefs, sea-grass meadow habitat and structures colonised with macroalgae, which they use for camouflage.

Amazing adaptations and morphology

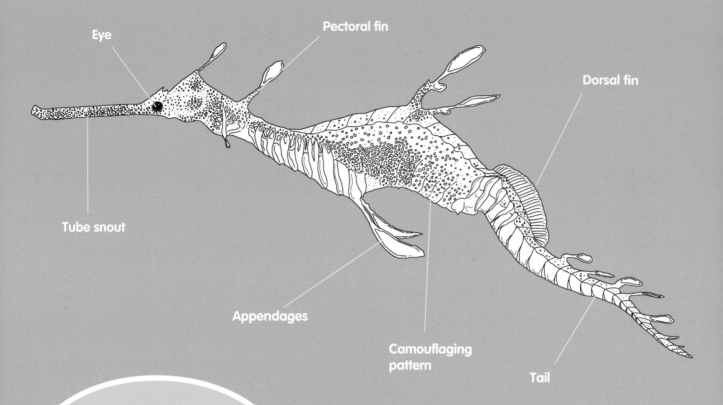

Eye

Pectoral fin

Dorsal fin

Tube snout

Appendages

Camouflaging pattern

Tail

The Weedy Seadragon is without teeth and lacks a stomach. They spend most of their lives continuously eating.

They are **carnivorous**, which means that they eat meat. They dine on a smorgasbord of small crustaceans such has krill, sea lice, fish larvae and mysid shrimps, sucking up their prey with expert precision using their long cylindrical snout.

The Weedy Seadragon can expand a joint in the lower jaw to enable it to change the aperture of the mouth opening, to accommodate different sizes of prey.

Usually solitary, these seadragons move to deeper waters over the cooler winter period when food is hard to find. As the seasons change, and the water temperature becomes warmer, the seadragons congregate in shallow waters to find a mate and to breed.

Unlike most fish that we are more familiar with, Weedy Seadragons are covered in a **tough outer skin**. The thick skin and small spines afford good protection from attack by predators. However, the armour-plated body impedes movement and speed.

Lacking a caudal fin, Weedy Seadragons are not graceful ocean swimmers. They propel themselves through the water by quickly oscillating their ventral and dorsal fins, changing depth and orientation using air bladders.

They remind me of an underwater hovercraft.

The swim bladders of Weedy Seadragons are extremely fragile. Sudden changes in water pressure or violent seas can cause the air bladders to burst, killing the fish. Dead Weedy Seadragons are often washed up on beaches after rough seas.

Just like people, Weedy Seadragons don't look alike. Age, environmental conditions, depth and habitat can change their colour and appearance.

WOW, did you know that scientists have discovered that individual specimens have distinct and recognisable facial patterns, like people having unique fingerprints?

A Weedy Seadragon's fins are small and translucent. These fish are extremely slow swimming and rely on their superb camouflage to evade predators.

One Weedy Seadragon has been clocked at a world-record beating 150 metres per hour!

The dorsal fins of this fish mimic the gas-filled floats known as pneumatocysts on kelp macro algae. The seadragon is covered in rings and patterns, which help to break up the outline of its long body in kelp forests and sea-grass meadows.

Wow, that really is an amazing master of disguise – with matching accessories!

Life cycle

The Weedy Seadragon usually reaches reproductive maturity after two years, once they are fully grown. Summertime heralds the breeding season for the Weedy Seadragon.

Weedy Seadragons are oviparous, which means that they lay eggs. One brood of eggs is laid each breeding season.

As with seahorses, Weedy Seadragon males are responsible for childbirth. But instead of a pouch, male seadragons have a spongy **brood patch** on the underside of their tail where females deposit their fluorescent pink eggs.

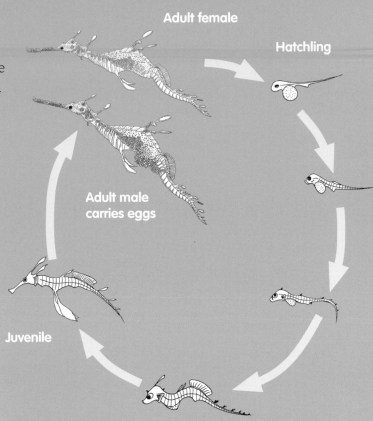

Adult female

Hatchling

Adult male carries eggs

Juvenile

> The male's skin on his tail is soft and spongy and forms a cup around each egg to keep the eggs nice and safe – it's like *Daddy Day Care*.

The Weedy Seadragon eggs are fertilised during the transfer from the female to the male. The male protects and incubates the eggs and carries them to full-term, releasing miniature seadragons into the ocean after about six to eight weeks.

> The female can lay up to a whopping 300 eggs.

The adult Weedy Seadragon offers no paternal care for his young. The baby **fry** hatch without leafy appendages and seek refuge in macro algae, where they are safe from hungry predators. The fry survive from their egg yolk for the first couple of days, until their snouts become more elongated so that they can feed on small zooplankton.

Predators and threats

Rays, seabirds, seals and sharks all predate upon Weedy Seadragons.

Weedy Seadragons are fully protected in all Australian waters. It is illegal to take them from their natural habitat. Habitat degradation by people is the biggest threat to wild seadragons.

The Weedy Seadragon is at risk of disappearing. The destruction of sea-grass beds and rocky reefs directly affects its future. Weedy Seadragons are poor dispersers, and do not have the ability to migrate and move great distances if their habitat is disturbed.

The IUCN red list recognises the Weedy Seadragons as 'Near Threatened' due to habitat loss and the adverse effects of climate change.

How can we help Weedy Seadragons?

Do your best to recycle and use environmentally friendly cleaning products and chemicals around the home.

Join a citizen-science program and report your observations and the locations of wild Weedy Seadragon populations.

If you are lucky enough to observe a wild Weedy Seadragon in its natural environment, look but don't touch; these are fragile animals and physical contact can be deleterious to their health.

Index

First published in 2023 by Reed New Holland Publishers
Sydney

Level 1, 178 Fox Valley Road, Wahroonga, NSW 2076, Australia

newhollandpublishers.com

Copyright © 2023 Reed New Holland Publishers
Copyright © 2023 in text: Chris Humfrey
Copyright © 2023 in maps and artworks: Lily Tomkinson
Copyright © 2023 in photographs: Jay Town

A record of this book is held at the National Library of Australia.

ISBN 978 1 76079 446 0

Managing Director: Fiona Schultz
Publisher and Project Editor: Simon Papps
Designer: Andrew Davies
Production Director: Arlene Gippert

Printed in China

10 9 8 7 6 5 4 3 2 1

Chris Humfrey's Awesome Australian Animals
ISBN 978 1 92554 670 5

Chris Humfrey's Coolest Creepy Crawlies
ISBN 978 1 76079 445 3

Colour With Chris Humfrey's Awesome Australian Animals
ISBN 978 1 76079 424 8

Colour With Chris Humfrey's Coolest Creepy Crawlies
ISBN 978 1 76079 546 7

For details of hundreds of other Natural History titles see newhollandpublishers.com

And keep up with New Holland Publishers:

NewHollandPublishers and ReedNewHolland

@newhollandpublishers